TREASURE ISLANDS
of the Inner Hebrides

A Traveller's Guide

Companion volumes
SKYE – A Traveller's Guide
MULL – A Traveller's Guide

TREASURE ISLANDS

of the Inner Hebrides

A Traveller's Guide

Christine Wiener

S. Forsyth, London

©1992 C. WIENER

Illustrations and Maps by Sophie Mason
Photographs by author
Typeset by Fakenham Photosetting Ltd,
Fakenham, Norfolk
Printed by The Iceni Press, Fakenham, Norfolk
Bound by J W Braithwaite and Son Ltd,
Wolverhampton

Published by Stuart Forsyth, 27 Longton Avenue,
London SE26 6RE

ISBN 0–9515476–2–3

Cover illustration: Breachachadh Castle

Table of Contents

The Cuillins of Skye

Kidalton Chapel (Islay)

The 'Little Cross' – Oronsay Priory

I

Roads to The Isles (1) – More about Oban

The evening train from Glasgow drawing into the station at Connel provides its passengers with their first sight of the mountains of Mull across the Firth of Lorn. As the sun sinks behind Morvern, Connel bridge stands out in silhouette, black on liquid gold. The long journey is nearly over now; the bridge is the last landmark before Oban. It was built in 1903 across the narrow mouth of Loch Etive downstream from the Falls of Lora to replace the ferry which had saved a detour of about forty miles round the lonely loch and had given its name to the town, Connel Ferry as it was then known. Connel faces the island of Lismore and on the sea trip there and back from Oban, the bridge re-appears, its delicate tracery silver against a backdrop of mountains in the mighty Ben Nevis range. Constructed of steel and stone on the cantilever system, it was modelled on the famous bridge spanning the Firth of Forth which celebrated its centenary in 1990.

It is fitting to arrive in Oban by train since it was the coming of the railway to the West Coast which confirmed the town's growing prosperity. Soon Oban was known as 'the Charing Cross of the North'. It has also been called 'the gateway to the Highlands', but the gate was hardly ajar before the railway boom of the 1840s. A short line – the Glasgow and Greenock Railway – was opened as early as 1831; on the east coast railway lines reached Perth and Aberdeen in 1848; by 1865, the various private companies known for their green and gold coaches had merged to form the Highland Railways. From 1880 onwards trains ran as far north as Mallaig and the Kyle of Lochalsh and the network included the Caledonian Railway, with branches to Ballachulish and Oban.

Oban received the royal accolade when the young Queen Victoria visited it in 1847. Her journey was made by water, in the Royal Yacht which anchored offshore to carefully orchestrated public acclaim at a time when Her Majesty's loyal subjects were being evicted to make room for sheep. The Queen's tour started from Inveraray where the Duke of Argyll had given her a truly royal welcome. From the castle, she set off down Loch Fyne to the head of the Crinan Canal, where a horse-drawn barge 'most magnificently decorated', she tells us, awaited her party. Once through the Canal's fifteen lochs and back on board the Royal Yacht, they sailed up through the waters of Lorn, past Jura and Scarba and through the narrow Sound of Luing up to the mouth of Loch Linnhe where they moored outside Oban on the 20th August. All along the way, royal salutes were fired from the shore and beacons were lighted on the hills. The Queen's visit to her Hebridean possessions ended with a trip up the Sound of Mull, past Duart Castle, past

Tobermory where again she did not land. From the headland of Ardnamurchan, it was just possible to see the mountains of Skye before the yacht rounded the northern end of Mull and turned down towards Staffa, where the Queen, the Prince Consort and the children were rowed to the entrance of Fingal's Cave. It was the nearest they got to setting foot in the Western Isles. The Queen thoroughly enjoyed herself, recording her delight in the scenery in rapturous clichés. She also expressed great pleasure in the enthusiastic welcome she received from the Highlanders gathered along her route. It seems she had been successfully shielded from the disaffected and knew nothing of the resentments of the dispossessed.

The Queen left her mark on Oban which remains very much a Victorian town – trim, orderly, active and prosperous. The famous Caledonian-Macbrayne ferries – Cal-Mac for short – anchor along the station pier, pleasure craft swing in the generally calm waters of the bay, the fishing fleet carries on its business amid the bustle of the warehouses. Shop windows gleam along the waterfront, there is a constant to-and-fro between the station, the landing-stage and the hotels, and the long esplanade, the Corran, is crowded with tourists enjoying the magnificent views over the island of Kerrera, which lies astride Oban Bay, across to Mull and the Morvern coast. Oban has been brought up to date, providing for its residents and its visitors all the current amenities. But apart from the Roman Catholic cathedral on the esplanade, built of pink granite in 1923 to the designs of Gilbert Scott, modern buildings merge into the background, subdued by their solid, if sometimes florid, nineteenth century neighbours. The whole is crowned by a truly Victorian enterprise: a miniature model of the Colosseum at Rome, known as McCaig's Tower. Though Queen Victoria had never heard of the Year of the Sheep, nor of the warning given in Gaelic as, '*mo thruaighe ort a thir, tha'n caoirach mhor a'teach'd*' – 'Woe to thee o land, the Great Sheep is coming' – one at least of her subjects, a prosperous and philanthropic banker called John Stuart McCaig, had witnessed the results in terms of unemployment. He lived to see the hordes of evicted crofters pouring down from the north in search of work in Glasgow and the ports of the West Coast. In 1897 he attempted to provide them with building work while erecting the extraordinary monument to his own name. A mausoleum was planned, and a tower a hundred feet high, but McCaig died before they were completed.

A guide book written not long after described Oban as 'a handsome and thriving modern town and the most fashionable of Scottish watering-places.' Earlier visitors to the Western Isles travelled less for enjoyment than for practical ends: Martin Martin, who had reached Mull and some of the Outer Islands by Queen Anne's day, ends his 'Description of the Western Islands of Scotland' with 'A Brief Account of the Advan-

4

tages the Isles afforded by Sea and Land, and particularly for a Fishing Trade'; later, John Knox, another Scotsman, who had made his fortune as a London bookseller, attempted to chart the seas on behalf of the British Society for Extending the Fisheries, founded in 1786. It was largely curiosity which, some ten years earlier, made Dr Johnson yield at last to Boswell's persuasion and visit Scotland. Both men left accounts of their journeyings – 'A Journey to the Western Islands of Scotland' by Johnson and 'The Journal of a Tour of the Hebrides' by his companion and biographer. This was still terra incognita – not only unknown but neglected. In his 'Tour Through the Whole Island of Great Britain', first published between 1724 and 1727, Daniel Defoe limited his comments on the Inner Hebrides to a brief mention of Skye and the few lines which close the third and final volume of his work: 'Off the western shore of Argyle and Lorn there are abundance of islands, which all belong to the family of Argyle, or at least to its jurisdiction, as Isla, Jura, Tyray, Lysmore, Coll and several others of less note.' In the intervening years, nothing much had changed: the Hebrides remained beneath the notice not only of the English, but of the Lowland Scots, as Dr Johnson noted, 'To the southern inhabitants of Scotland, the state of the mountains and the islands is equally unknown with that of Borneo or Sumatra: of both they have only heard a little, and guess the rest.' While Boswell's chief concern was with recording the sayings of his famous friend, Johnson's acute eye caught the details of daily life. Nor did the state of the economy – ruined landlords and increasingly insecure tenants – escape his notice. He thought on these things, examined their causes, and was well ahead of his time in some of the solutions he suggested and some of those he rejected. Yet both Johnson and Boswell belonged to their day, and what startles the modern reader is the nearly total absence in their books of any reference to the magnificent scenery which constantly surrounded them during the four months they spent in Scotland. The simple explanation is that nature in the raw had no appeal during most of the eighteenth century – its hardships were endured, its beauties overlooked. Practically the sole comment Dr Johnson made about Oban was that it had 'a tolerable inn', the practical comforts of which affected him far more than the intangible beauty of the bay and its setting.

But the Age of Enlightenment was giving way to the Age of Sensibility and Walter Scott was soon to sell 'Caledonia stern and wild' to the public at large. His 'Minstrelsy of the Scottish Border', published in 1802 and soon followed by 'The Lay of the Last Minstrel', introduced his rapidly growing readership to their past, a past set amid the rugged grandeur of mountain, moor and loch. 'The Lady of the Lake' of 1810 confirmed the growing appeal of the Highlands: it was a runaway success and it sent tourists in their hundreds to see for themselves Loch Katrine, and Ellen's Isle, the Silver Strand and the Goblin's Cave and the glen known as the Pass of the Cattle. Here, towering over the lake were the high peaks of Ben Venue and Ben Aan with, 'crags, and knolls, and mounds confusedly hurled, the fragments of an earlier world', scenery very different from the tamed landscape to which the new breed of travellers had been accustomed. It was, in Wordsworth's words, 'untouched, unbreathed upon' – and they loved it. Before long, 'doing' the Trossachs was more fashionable than the Grand Tour of the Continent. Even so, the parties who came to Loch Katrine were shy of venturing further. Dorothy Wordsworth, who accompanied her brother on their first visit to the district, was amused to meet a lady on the shores of the loch who was shocked and amazed to hear that they intended travelling west. Nor were such fears entirely fanciful: they may have been exaggerated but the hardships were real enough. The Wordsworths had experienced most of them during their first tour, made in 1803 before the Scottish craze began and which ended suitably enough with a meeting in the Borders with Walter Scott whose work Wordsworth already greatly admired. Travel in the border country was easier, but in the Highlands the Wordsworths had often been soaked in their open jaunting car and they had had a nasty accident when they were overthrown on a rocky road. Accommodation was poor, far below the standard of England's coaching inns; travellers often slept in wet

Dunollie Castle

sheets, sometimes they went hungry, occasionally they were turned away to spend the night on the open moor. But the Wordsworths persisted and reached Oban. They visited Dunollie Castle and William recorded his indignation in a poem to a caged eagle kept there. From this first visit to Scotland (another was made in 1814 as far north as Inverness) William also brought back the memory of the Highland lass who 'sang of old, unhappy far off things/ And battles long ago' while Dorothy kept a diary later published as 'Recollections of a Tour Made in Scotland.'

Their friend, Samuel Taylor Coleridge, had accompanied the Wordsworths for part of the way; other poets, notably John Keats, were soon to follow suit, and a host of painters, writers and musicians embarked on

what was becoming a pilgrimage to the Isles. Though he was dying of consumption, Keats walked the final 15 miles to Oban to take ship to Mull, which Robert Louis Stevenson was to use as the setting for several episodes of his novel, 'Kidnapped'. But perhaps it was the young Felix Mendelssohn who, in 1829, best encapsulated the mood of the Romantic Revival with his 'Hebrides Overture' written after exploring Fingal's Cave on Staffa which had been 'discovered' only recently and practically by accident by the explorer, Joseph Banks. As for Walter Scott, hoping to repeat the success of the 'Lady of the Lake', he set out by sea to travel the Hebrides in search of local colour for the new epic he was planning. But when 'The Lord of the Isles' appeared, the public did not take to it. 'Waverley', on the other hand, which was published anonymously, was an instant best-seller and it was quickly followed by such favourites as 'Guy Mannering' and 'Rob Roy'. The Waverley novels completed the work started by Walter Scott's poetry and put Scotland firmly on the tourist map.

By now, travel was becoming easier, with steamboats plying a regular trade from Glasgow. The *Comet* – the first sea-going vessel powered by steam – made its appearance in Loch Linnhe in 1820, some ten years after Henry Bell built its prototype. Already in 1812, his 'puffer' operated on the Clyde, bringing crowds to Helensburgh which provided rich Glasgow merchants with all the pleasures of a sea-side resort. Helensburgh has recognised its debt to Henry Bell – a fine granite obelisk stands on the Esplanade. Now it was possible – weather and tides permitting – to travel the 170 miles or so to Fort William in under three days. The press took up the story, marvelling at the speed modern technology was providing. It ignored the dangers. In the winter of 1820 – the year of its first trip north – the *Comet* foundered on the return journey from Fort William. Snow was falling as she left Oban, and in poor visibility she hit the rocks off the north of Jura. On this occasion, passengers and crew were able to clamber ashore, but the ship split in two and part of it was swept off into the Corryvreckan whirlpool. However, the engine was salvaged and a new, much larger *Comet* was built in the docks at Dumbarton. Soon a regular service was established not only to Fort William, but through the newly-opened Caledonian Canal as far as Inverness. But in 1825, on the way back from the east coast, the *Comet* was involved in a collision near the entrance to the Clyde. This time, seventy lives were lost. There were those who christened the *Comet* the Devil's engine and it is said that when she made her first appearance in the Hebrides, the natives fled in terror at the sight of this novel sea-monster billowing smoke. But travel by steamship had come to stay – after all, the new vessels were no more dangerous than the open sailing boats which had preceded them.

It was in the year that the second Comet sank that an English fan of the Waverley novels, J. E. Bowman, embarked in Glasgow with his companion, J. F. M. Dovaston, at the start of a summer expedition through the Highlands and Islands. The entry in Bowman's diary for Wednesday 20th July reads as follows: 'We rose early, and at six o'clock got aboard the Marion Steam Packet at the Broomielaw, a long modern quay, at the west end of Glasgow, where all the vessels belonging to the port, have their station. Fifteen years ago, vessels of 50 tons could not approach Glasgow, on account of the shallowness of the water; but so much attention has been paid to the deepening and embanking of the river, that vessels of 250 tons burden can now lie at the quay.' Even the second *Comet* weighed less than 100 tons. On this sea-voyage, the two friends, the Banker and the Barrister as they playfully referred to themselves, went no further than Dumbarton, and from there continued overland to the banks of Loch Lomond to board another steamer which took them up through the lake and its many islands as far north as Tarbet. The return journey was made from Arrochar, at the head of Loch Long where the *St Columba* 'fitted up with extreme elegance' took them back south to Clydeside. There were five days left till they sailed to their next destination – the isle of Mull where they intended to embark for Staffa and Iona. The intervening time was spent in visiting Inveraray and the Trossachs, with the now compulsory trip to Loch Katrine, where Bowman paid his tri-

The Old Forest

bute to Walter Scott. 'Of all the fairy scenes that Scotland has hitherto presented to our observation, the Trossachs and Loch Katrine must undoubtedly be set down as the most enchanting. Who that has a mind the least sensible to the charms of Nature and Poetry, cannot fail, while rambling here, to bear testimony to the spirited fidelity of the picture that Sir W. Scott has drawn of it.'

The 26th July found the two friends back in Glasgow again hurrying down to the Broomielaw where they 'got on deck just as the Bagpipes gave the signal . . . to get under weigh'. The vessel was the Highlander Steam Packet bound for the Hebrides. So far the weather had been fine and hot and it continued so as they made their way down to the coast, over to Rothesay on the isle of Bute, then through the Kyles and across 'noble Loch Fyne' to the Crinan Canal. The next morning found them in the Sound of Jura breakfasting off fresh herrings; as they made their way past Scarba, the dread Corryvreckan was pointed out to them, and Bowman wrote, 'there is more real danger comprized in one day's sailing in a boat among these islands, than in a whole East India voyage.' But they reached the waters of Lorn safely, passed Kerrera, admiring the fine views of Mull, Morvern and Appin, and turned south of Lismore to land on Mull. Oban they visited on the return journey, and Bowman wrote in praise of 'the lovely little town'. He was quick to appreciate its natural advantages: 'It is sufficiently extensive to afford anchorage to five-hundred sail of vessels and is well defended from the western winds.' Though he spent only a few hours in Oban before boarding the *Ben Nevis* en route for Fort William, he learnt something of the town's development. At the time Bowman was there, it was said to contain one-thousand inhabitants, 'mostly employed in the fisheries and coasting trade', living in houses 'modern and white-washed'. According to some authorities, Oban was no more than a small village in 1800 – a string of cottages along the foreshore – and in the days of Johnson's 'tolerable inn' had only one building worthy of being called a house. 'The first house of any consequence', Bowman wrote, 'was built about fifty years ago by a trading company at Renfrew, who used it as a storeroom. The example being followed by other mercantile adventurers, Oban soon became a considerable place, and about ten years subsequent to its first foundation, was made one of the ports belonging to the Customs house.'

Nothing much is left of Oban as Bowman saw it, not even the Customs house itself. Erected *circa* 1765. it was pulled down when the railway came to Oban. One link with the Customs, however, remains – the Oban distillery, built in 1794 by the Stevenson family, the two orphaned sons of a local stonemason to whose 'spirited exertions', Bowman said, Oban was much indebted. Oban distillery has now had nearly two hundred years experience; its malt is easy to recognise in its distinctive bottle shaped like a decanter. The art of distilling whisky is an ancient one – Scotland probably owes it to the early monks. But the trade remained largely outside the law until the nineteenth century. The first attempts (1707) to regulate the making and selling of whisky were generally ignored: the ingredients – barley, pure water and peat – were at hand; the terrain was favourable for setting up illicit stills, which were hidden in the folds of the moors, and smugglers had little difficulty evading the patrol boats and landing untaxed whisky (as well as French wines and brandy) in the innumerable creeks and coves along the coast. It was not until 1823 that an Act of Parliament prompted by the Duke of Gordon gradually brought the moonlighters to order and their profits, to the Revenue. Whisky would not have been part of the creature comforts Johnson and Boswell enjoyed at the Oban inn. The 'water of life' belonged to the bothy, it was claret that the gentry took at the laird's table. Johnson apparently tasted whisky only once, downing a dram offered in a 'hut' on the banks of Loch Ness. Good food and sound bedding were no doubt provided at the inn, but it was the regained sense of freedom that the returned travellers relished. As Boswell put it, 'After having been so long confined at different times in the islands, from which it was always uncertain when we could get away, it was comfortable to be now on the main land, and to know that, if in health, we might get to any place in Scotland or England in a certain number of days.'

O   5

MILES
APPROX

LISMORE

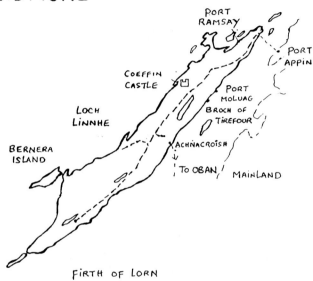

PORT
RAMSAY

PORT
APPIN

COEFFIN
CASTLE

PORT
MOLUAG

BROCH OF
TIREFOUR

LOCH
LINNHE

ACHNACROISH

BERNERA
ISLAND

TO OBAN   MAINLAND

FIRTH OF LORN

OBAN

CARN
BREUGACH

SLATERICH

THE
HORSESHOES

GYLEN
CASTLE

MAINLAND

KERRERA

II

. . . And its Outliers, Kerrera and Lismore

Modern travel has done away with the anxieties and incertitudes suffered by Boswell and his contemporaries. Plans can be made and the strictest schedule adhered to – witness the overnight coach parties who pour out of the hotels to board their 'buses in the morning. However remote their destination, the chances are that they will reach it on time. The tourist trail is far longer, but with speed at a premium, there is less opportunity to become acquainted with the stopping places along the route, less time to stand and stare. Travelling hopefully has given way to arriving at the appointed time. Something gained, something lost, and with far less excuse than their predecessors, too many visitors to the West Coast still neglect Oban, treating it merely as a ferry port to some of their favourite islands, since it provides a regular and frequent service to Mull, with access to Iona and Staffa, sailings to Coll and Tiree, sailings to Colonsay and further off, to South Uist and Barra in the Outer Hebrides. Amid the bustle of arrivals and departures, it is easy to overlook two islands much closer at hand, Kerrera and Lismore, where nothing much happens and time slips back easily into the past.

Kerrera's chief link with modern Oban is the fine obelisk at the north end which com-

memorates David Hutcheson, senior partner in the firm which was to become Caledonian–MacBrayne. Kerrera now has its own service which recalls the old days when ferrymen had no regular time-table – a motor-boat slips over the half-mile stretch of water to Horse-shoe Bay practically on demand. One of its most regular passengers is the village school-teacher who lives on the mainland. The island, which is about five miles long and two miles at its widest, remains much as it was when cattle was swum over to find extra pas-ture and drovers used it as a staging-post on their way to the trysts in the South. The modern age is represented in the north by a

fishing and packing station and a small ship-
yard. There the land is green and low-lying;
the south grows wilder and rocky, with Carn
Breugach, which overlooks Little Horseshoe
Bay a mile down the coast from the landing
stage, rising to over six hundred feet. History
has not passed Kerrera by: it has, for instance,
its own associations with the first Jacobite rising when one of the firmest supporters of the
exiled king lay hidden in the district. After the
failure of the '15, Ian Ciar (Swarthy John)
MacDougall took shelter in one of the many
caves along the Sound of Kerrera. Provisions
were brought to him from the island, and, on
dark nights, he was occasionally able to meet

his wife, Mary, at a house in the small township of Slaterich. Ian Ciar spent long years in exile before he was pardoned in 1729; during the '45 and Bonnie Prince Charlie's wanderings, his son Alexander, who had married a Campbell from the opposite camp, stayed at home. But the MacDougalls' links with Kerrera go back much further than the Risings, for it was at their castle of Gylen that the famous trophy, known as the Brooch of Lorn, was kept. The brooch came into the MacDougalls' possession during a battle fought in 1308 at the Pass of Brander, between Loch Etive and Loch Awe, when Robert the Bruce came near to capture. Walter Scott recounts in dramatic detail how he was surrounded and fought free amid the swirling mists falling from the mountains and rising from the waters of the lakes below. Followers of the MacDougalls (then known as the Lords of Lorn), a father and his two sons called MacAndrossen closed in on the king, one son seizing the reins, the other grabbing him by the legs to pull him from the saddle. Both were cut down. Then, 'the father, seeing his two sons thus slain, flew desperately at the King, and grasped him by the mantle so close to his body, that he could not have room to wield his big sword. But with the heavy pommel of that weapon, or, as others say, with an iron hammer which hung at his saddle-bow, the King struck so dreadful a blow that he dashed out his brains. Still, however, the Highlander kept his dying grasp on the King's mantle; so that, to be free of the dead body, Bruce was obliged to undo his brooch, or clasp, by which it was fastened, and leave that, and the mantle itself, behind him.' Walter Scott adds: 'the brooch, which fell thus into the possession of MacDougall of Lorn, is still preserved in that ancient family, as a memorial that the celebrated Bruce once narrowly escaped falling into the hands of their ancestor'. Later, the brooch disappeared, probably stolen by Covenanters who invaded and sacked Gylen in 1647. It was recovered in the 19th century and returned to the MacDougalls who kept it in Dunollie Castle.

Gylen Castle stands in the south-east corner of Kerrera, past Little Horseshoe Bay. It is now in ruins, but the ruins are substantial and very impressive. They are described in Nigel Tranter's guide to Argyll and Bute: 'A tall, slender L-planned tower, with a tiny courtyard to the south, it rises four storeys in the main block with the stair-wing a storey higher to end in a gabled watch-chamber reached by a circular turret-stair. The main roof is crowstepped – gabled with an angle-turret. Machicolated projections for defensive dropping are provided at various points, and there are numerous shot-holes and gunloops. The entrance is unusual, the bar-holed doorway facing north, with a vaulted passage running through the main-block basement to give access to the courtyard. Here another defensive door opens on to the stair-wing.' The present structure, what is left of it, goes back to *circa* 1528, the official date, but other authorities describe Gylen as a Norwegian fortress, which given its strategically important position seems likely enough. Though it came to serve the MacDougalls as a summer residence, the site was surely first chosen to oversee the southern approaches of the Sound of Kerrera as Dunollie guards the north.

The Sound of Kerrera has seen much historic traffic: King Haakon of Norway sailed through it, and anchored at Little Horseshoe Bay, on his way to battle and defeat at Largs in 1263. And it was between the two Horseshoe Bays that, a few years earlier, Alexander the Second was carried ashore to die – some say of poison – at a spot still known as the King's Well. The King was preparing a campaign against Ewen, Lord of Argyll, who was in league with the Norsemen occupying the Western Isles when he was struck down by a fever. In the days when the causes of ailments were unknown and their symptoms went unrecognised, "holy water" was often medicine's only resort. The king drank the water of Kerrera's well, the king died – and there was nothing unusual in that.

Miraculous properties have been ascribed to wells and springs since the earliest times, in Scotland as elsewhere. In the Hebrides, waters with special curative powers proliferate – wells long worshipped are to be found in Skye, Islay, Jura, Gigha and Eigg among others. Martin described several, including the one in the curiously named village of Fivepennies on Eigg which he was told, 'never fails to cure any Person of his first Disease, only by drinking a Quantity of it for the space of two or three days'. In Skye, he came across a well near Kilbride considered to provide a universal panacea. It contained 'one Trout only in it; the Natives are very tender of it, and tho they often chance to catch it in their wooden Pales, they are very careful to preserve it from being destroy'd'. On Colonsay, no less than forty wells have been listed, which seems excessive for an island less than ten miles long. A quasi-religious feeling for the forces of nature is held in common by all primitive peoples, and given the character of the lands they occupied, it is hardly surprising that the Celts in particular should have been pre-occupied with water. As Dr Grant (*Highland Folk Ways*) sees it, well worship is one of the most understandable of early cults for 'as one watches the water of a mountain spring bubbling out of the ground, the grains of sand in the little basin it has made for itself, dancing in the flow of water, it is easy to imagine that some mysterious power is immanent in it'. Before the gods came, earthly spirits were firmly enthroned, and the Druids had to come to terms with them; the Christian missionaries followed suit, taking over sites held sacred and baptizing them, as it were, by the names of the saints of the Church. Another healing well in Skye is known as St Katharine's; on Colonsay, the well dedicated to St Oran, a contemporary of St Columba, is preserved in the grounds of Colonsay House; on Kerrera, tradition has it that St. Maelrubha, another early missionary, set up a

cashel, as the rudimentary monasteries of the
Celtic church were known, somewhere in the
vicinity of the sacred well. St Columba himself was involved in the take-over of wells, as
Adamnan, one of his first biographers,
relates. 'There was a foundation famous
among this heathen people (the northern
Picts), which foolish men, having their senses
blinded by the devil, worshipped as a God . . .
and paid divine honour to the fountain.' It
seems that fear rather than faith was the
motive, for all who drank from it, or washed
in it, were afflicted with leprosy or other ills.
Fearlessly, Columba put himself to the test
watched by the Druids. 'Having first raised
his holy hand and invoked the names of
Christ, (he) washed his hands and feet; and
then with his companions, drank of the water
which he had blessed.' And from that day the
demons departed from the fountain where
water henceforth served to cure the ills it had
formerly inflicted. The Church was well
acquainted with the devil; the pagans were
well aware of the ambivalent quality of the
powers they served. Nature was moody, and
so were its deities – the sea that fed the
islanders also killed its fishermen. Bell, book
and candle – in Columba's day an invocation
or a sign of the cross – disposed of evil spirits;
earlier elaborate rituals grew up to propitiate
fickle gods. Ancient rituals outlast the generations and have a habit of surviving in folk
tradition long after their original significance
has been lost. Animal sacrifices were replaced
in time by gifts of food to the demi-gods, and

24

there is something left of pagan practice in the pennies dropped in wishing-wells today.

Saints and holy wells have their place in the history of Lismore, or at any rate in the legends that surround the island, which lies at the confluence of the Firth of Lorn, the Sound of Mull and Loch Linnhe. Green and exceptionally fertile, its Gaelic name means 'the great garden', though there are some who translate 'lios mor' as 'the sacred enclosure', which is how St Moluag regarded the island, his parish. As the story goes, St Columba and St Moluag competed to establish a mission on Lismore and decided to settle their differences by a trial of strength. Having agreed that whoever first touched land should take possession, they set out in rowing boats and raced for Lismore. As they drew near, St Moluag was falling back, but he won the day by his wits. Seeing St Columba about to beach, he drew out his dirk and cutting off his little finger, threw it ashore – thus being the first to 'land'. Or so the story goes. However he got there, St Moluag made Lismore his headquarters and left his imprint on the island, where he lived out his life and died in 592. His arrival is remembered in the cove on the east coast called after him Port Moluag, where he is believed to have landed. A whiff of the miraculous surrounds a great scooped-out boulder nearby where the saint would rest on his journeyings through the island: it is know as Moluag's Chair and sufferers from rheumatism who sit in it are relieved of their pains. There is nothing left of Moluag's original foundation near Clachan. It was called Kilmoluag and it had its day in the thirteenth century when it was raised to the dignity of a Roman Catholic Cathedral. That was burnt down during the Reformation and the small whitewashed church built in the grave-yard is the sole remaining token of former glory. A so-called Sanctuary Stone by the roadside nearby certainly suggests ancient holy ground.

Another relic of St Moluag is preserved – his pastoral staff known as Bachuil Mor, a blackthorn stick which is assumed to have served him as the bishop's crozier of later days. As was the custom, the staff was given its own guardians, or dewars. The office was held by clan MacLeary (also called Macdon-leavy), kin to the ancient and powerful Buchanan family. Apart from being custo-dians of the staff – which earned them the title of Barons of the Bachuil – the MacLearys have another claim to fame: under their angli-cized name of Livingstone, they are the ances-tors of the Victorian explorer, David Liv-ingstone. The Bachuil is now kept at Inveraray Castle; in common with objects and places associated with Scotland's earliest saints, it is credited with supernatural powers. St Moluag's aura pervades Lismore as St Col-umba's does Iona; he has his healing well near where he landed. St Andrew, Scotland's patron saint, has one too, a spring by the shores of Loch Balnagowan. The well that St Columba 'converted' was somewhere in the north, near Inverness perhaps; in Lismore, he is remembered not by water but by wood. He has his special corner in the tiny offshore island of Bernera down in the south-west corner, which can be reached on foot – just about – at low tide. There are traces of an ancient chapel which tradition ascribes to Columba, and there is his yew under which a thousand people could gather to hear him preach. The yew was a sacred tree in Ireland, and it was the custom to plant yews close by the house where they served as 'lord of the home', as well as in graveyards to turn away the returning spirit of the dead. Like the rowan, the magic of the yew could work for good or ill – cutting it down was held to bring bad luck. To Columba, the Bernera yew was sacred – he put a curse on anyone who injured it. The tree lived on until in the eighteenth century, a Campbell laird of Benderloch, who was rebuilding his mansion, had it chopped down to make a new staircase. A series of disasters ensued – a tree-feller was killed, several of the boatmen shipping the timber to the mainland were drowned; then the laird died and the house burned down. Today, all that remains of old Lochnell House is a gutted wing, and of the tree, some hopeful offshoots.

The dividing line between superstition and religious belief is paper-thin; but the story of how yet another sacred spring came by its name belongs to the secular tradition. It all started across the Sound of Mull, in Tobermory where the wreck of the *Florida* (some call it the Florencia) lies under the silt eleven fathoms deep. Firm facts are few, but we do know that after the defeat of the Armada, the great Spanish galleon, driven off Islay, sought refuge in Tobermory where she blew up and sank. Some say the ship was set on fire through the agency of one of Queen Elizabeth's spies; others, that witchcraft was at work. The *Florida* may have been acting as the Armada's pay ship, loaded with bullion and coin; more to the romantic point, she had on board a precious cargo in the person of Doña Clara, the discontented daughter of a Spanish grandee. The young lady had turned down a long list of acceptable suitors after dreaming of a fair lover whom she was determined to seek out in the northern regions where he appeared to belong. So she became a passenger on the *Florida* (women aboard warships were not so unusual then) and met her fate in Lachlan Maclean of Duart when he came aboard to discuss approvisioning the Spaniards. It seems that he returned her love; at any rate, his frequent visits aroused the jealousy of his wife, Lady Margaret (Cunninghame) who took her revenge by sinking the ship. She sought the help of the great witch of Lochaber who released an army of cats to board the *Florida*. Once over the bulwarks, they scratched the crew to death, then set fire to the powder-keg, according to one version of the old tale. Doña Clara's body was washed ashore on Lismore where it was buried with the reverence due to a noble foreigner. But her spirit could not rest quiet. She appeared in a dream to Lachlan, demanding that her bones be disinterred and taken back

28

to Spain after being cleansed in the waters of the sacred spring – which has since been known as Clara's Well.

The sad little tale of Doña Clara and her dream lover echoes a much older story attached to Coeffin Castle on the west coast and belongs to the days of the Norse. Readily accessible and difficult to defend, Lismore was an obvious target for the spring hostings when the dragon ships of the Scandinavians descended on the Highlands and Islands. As a general rule these raids were seasonal, leaving behind them a thick cloud of smoke from the burning thatches, depleted fields from which the cattle had been stolen, ugly rows of decapitated heads, raped matrons and maidens, and only the very young and the very old left to mourn them. Occasionally permanent settlements were established and Coeffin among other remains suggests that this was the case on Lismore. The present ruins of the castle, standing on a rocky promontory with fine views over Loch Linnhe to the mountains of Morvern, belong to the thirteenth century when the MacDougalls of Lorn built up a substantial fortress on the site of an earlier structure, which is thought to have been the headquarters of a Norse chieftain named Chaifen. The link with Doña Clara lies with his sister, Bheothail. The young lady, who was affianced, died of grief on hearing that her lover had been killed on the field of a faraway battle. She was buried in the castle's precincts: the remains of a cist – the hollowed-out stone coffin of the day – on the

Achnacroish on Lismore

shore are thought to mark the spot. But her ghost returned to haunt her brother, demanding to be buried at her lover's side. So her remains, like Doña Clara's, were gathered up, washed clean in the sacred well and sent overseas. Yet the bards say the hauntings continued. At last, the grave on the shore was re-examined and a tiny bone which had been overlooked was discovered and sent off to join the skeletons united in the lovers' joint tomb. Then the hauntings ceased.

For so small an island, about ten miles long and seldom more than a mile across, Lismore has a great variety of ancient sites and remains, both from the Christian era and before. Prac-

tically opposite Coeffin Castle on the east
coast, for example, there stands the Pictish
hill-fort known as the Broch of Tirefour. On
a hill overlooking the sea, it is fairly well preserved. Lesser remains of another ancient
stronghold, Dun Guilean, are to be found in
the south-western half of the island, beyond
the ridge of Barr Mor. On the coast nearby,
approximately facing Bernera, there is a
monumental token to Lismore's Christian
past, a bishop's palace known as Achandun
Castle to match its cathedral. The building
with its ruined towers and fortifications,
which suggest secular as well as spiritual
power, belongs to the thirteenth century and

for three hundred years served as the Isles' episcopal seat, until early in the sixteenth century a new and more convenient residence was built on the mainland in Kintyre. Achnacroish, the ferry port from Oban, has its own past stretching back to early Christian times. Nowadays it is a neat, pretty village with some old cottages. Its name means the Field of the Cross and it is held to have been a burial site of Pictish kings. The seven-mile crossing from Oban takes an hour or so, an hour of unpolluted air between blue water and blue mountains; a shorter crossing made from Port Appin, further up the mainland coast, takes a matter of minutes. One disembarks at a jetty at the north end of Lismore, called appropriately, North Point. It is within easy reach of Port Ramsay, known as one of the best anchorages in the Hebrides and an important commercial centre when limestone was still quarried on Lismore.

There are a few disused lime kilns left standing south of Achnacroish but the trade was abandoned last century. It is lime, incidentally, which is held responsible for Lismore's fertility, its greenness, its masses of wildflowers. But appearances can be deceptive, and the richest natural resources can be defeated by economic developments. The lime industry given up, the trade in kelp coming to an end after the Napoleonic wars, the partial failure of attempts to establish a profitable fishing industry, enclosures and clearances meant that Lismore shared the fate of other islands – gradual depopulation. In 1800 it supported nearly two thousand souls; in 1977, fewer than one hundred and fifty people lived on Lismore. But its story will not be forgotten – it has been set down in the tremendous compilation of Gaelic lore recorded in 1512 by Sir James MacGregor, Notary Public and Dean of Lismore.

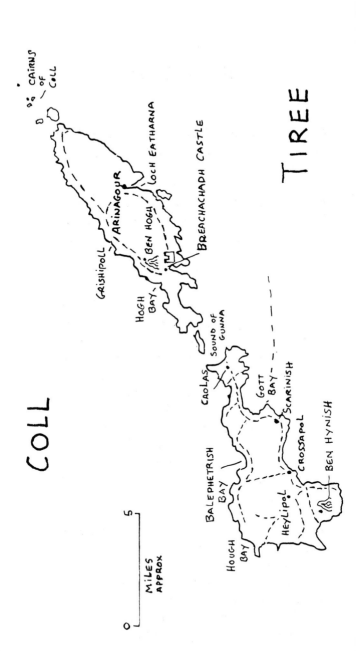

COLL

TIREE

CAIRNS
OF
COLL

GRISHIPOLL
ARINAGOUR
BEN HOGH
LOCH EATHARNA
BREACHACHADH CASTLE
HOGH BAY
Sound of GUNNA
CAOLAS
GOTT BAY
SCARINISH
BALEPHETRISH BAY
CROSSAPOL
BEN HYNISH
HEYLIPOL
HOUGH BAY

5

MILES
APPROX

0

III

Coll and Tiree

Where the Dean of Lismore made it his life's
work to collect records of the past, Dean
Munro wrote of his own day, of the people
and places he knew. The island of Coll, which
lies out at sea through the Sound of Mull he
described as very fertile, with one castle and
one parish church, good for fishermen and
fowlers, 'with ane utter fine Falcon nest in it'.
He also mentioned Gunna, the islet at Coll's
southern tip as 'manurit and inhabite, gude
for corn, store and fishing'. The Dean is even
more enthusiastic about the neighbouring
island of Tiree and its agricultural potential. A
most fertile and fruitful country, he calls it,
and goes on to say, 'Na cuntrie may be more
fertile of corn, and very good for wild fowls
and for fische'. Martin Martin, travelling
through the Hebrides towards the end of the
seventeenth century agreed with the Dean
that 'Tiree has always been valued for its
extraordinary Fruitfulness in Corn'. By then,
Tiree's reputation was already well established. In St Columba's day it is thought to
have served as Iona's granary, and there are
those who translate its name, in one of its
many spellings, as 'the land of corn'.

Both Coll and Tiree would have come
within Columba's parish: he himself is
recorded as having landed on Tiree in the year
565, and the monk Adamnan says two

monasteries were established there by his followers. If so, they would have been destroyed in Viking raids and the few traces they may have left is a matter for archaeologists. Adamnan also speaks of a mission to an island identified as Coll. At any rate, St Columba saw to it that Coll as well as Tiree should go free of snakes when he banned all reptiles from Iona, a privilege not extended to Mull.

If Tiree served as Iona's 'breadbasket', it was Coll's fishing ground which impressed Martin. There were trout and eels in profusion in the freshwater lake on the south-east side and, more importantly, along the coast cod and ling in abundance which Martin found 'of a larger size than in the adjacent Isles or Continent'.

Lying far out from the mainland, well on the way to the Outer Hebrides, Coll and Tiree have had more need than most to be self-supporting to survive, and this explains the emphasis travellers put on their natural resources. Grain – oats and barley and corn – formed the basis of the people's staple diet, from porridge to the many 'cakes' for which Scotland is still justly famous. Bread, especially white bread, was reserved for the gentry; in the shielings and on the moor, they ate the oatcakes which now appear as a luxury item on the nation's supermarket shelves. With most cattle sold on the hoof to be fattened up on richer grassland, fish took the place of meat, as well as providing oil for the 'crusies' that lit the dark interiors of the croft houses. Martin has a good tale of an unexpected catch of whale on Tiree: 'Some years ago, about one hundred and sixty little whales, the biggest not exceeding twenty foot long, ran themselves ashore in this Isle, very seasonably, in time of Scarcity, for the natives did eat them all; and told me that the Sea-Pork, i.e. the Whale, is both wholesome and very nourishing Meat.' As Dr Johnson was to observe during his tour of the Hebrides, 'If it were always practicable to fish, these Islands could never be in much danger of famine.' But in winter at the very time when provisions were running low, the seas were too heavy and the rocky coast too dangerous. Storm-bound on Coll, on his way from Skye to Mull, Dr Johnson had no time to visit Tiree, though he knew of its reputation as 'eminently fertile'. He was particularly well placed to study the island's economy for his host was Donald Maclean, 'Young Col', who had travelled to England to learn the most up-to-date farming methods and was determined to improve his patrimony as well as his tenants' lot. Some of his notions were fanciful – planting an orchard on land so exposed to the winds that there is hardly a tree to be seen. As Boswell said, 'We walked a little in the laird's garden, in which some endeavours have been used to rear some trees; but as soon as they got above the surrounding wall, they died.' But the laird had other plans that made sound sense, including the introduction of turnip crops for winter fodder. 'Young Col' was also responsible for importing the first

wheeled carts to travel the new road he started building from Breachachadh to Loch Eatherna. But good or bad, his 'improvements' came to nothing – just about a year after discussing his plans with Dr Johnson, he was drowned in a storm off Mull.

Once, in prehistoric times, Coll and Tiree were one island – they have so much in common that it sometimes seems that they still are. The narrow (2 miles) Sound of Gunna now separates them, but although Tiree lies a little to the south of Coll, from a distance they emerge as one extended, low-lying strip. They are much of a size – Coll, thirteen miles long to Tiree's eleven, and

about three miles across. Tiree's width ranges
from six miles in the south to no more than a
mile or two where innumerable bays and
inlets bite deeply into its coast. The islands
share the same soil and the same long
stretches of virgin sands; their coasts are dan-
gerously dotted with skerries, of which the
reefs known as the Cairns of Coll at the most
impressive as they are first seen south of Ardnamurchan Head. Bowman called them a
'cluster of cliffs' having the appearance of
'towering castles whose foundations lie buried beneath the waves.' Bowman also noted,
correctly, that Tiree lay lower in the water
than Coll – one of its ancient Gaelic names

means 'the kingdom whose summits are below the waves'. Coll and Tiree also have something in common with the Outer Hebrides, lying as they do unprotected from the seas and open to the winds. And like most of the Outer Isles, they come under the influence of the Gulf Stream which keeps their climate mild: Tiree has more hours of sunshine a year than practically any other place in Britain. And both islands have some of the finest machair in the Hebrides. In season, that is in the summer, it is knee-deep in wild flowers – buttercups, red and white clover, daisies, speedwell, dandelions, eyebright, birdsfoot trefoil and its relation known as hop-clover, harebell which is called the cuckoo's shoe in Gaelic, thyme, blue and yellow pansies, cornflowers known as Blue Bonnets, silverweed and several sorts of wild orchid. Through the ages, most of these common flowers (common that is before modern farming methods destroyed them) have been valued as curatives, serving as the people's medicine chest; others provided food. Thus the roots of silverweed (potentilla anserina) were eaten boiled or roasted before the introduction of the potato, and in time of scarcity, ground down to take the place of flour. Before the Second World War, six hundred and fifty varieties of wild flowers were listed in the Inner Hebrides and more than five hundred and seventy were found on Coll and Tiree, where they are still at less risk from chemical pollution than elsewhere in the British Isles.

Overlooking the machair and the beaches, there are hills to be climbed, for it is not quite true to call Coll and Tiree as flat as a pancake. The main height on Coll is Ben Hogh, which rises to 339 feet above the bay of the same name on the north-west coast across the island from Arinagour. Apart from providing magnificent views over the sands and out to sea, it has a curious geological feature – a huge shapeless rock which rests precariously on three smaller stones and appears to sway without ever toppling over. This oddity is no doubt the result of some volcanic upheaval during the Ice Age, but legend finds a prettier way of explaining it: a game played by a giant and his mistress using rocks as balls. Boswell got the story from Young Col as they were riding by, and he thought it worth recording: 'The tradition is, that a giant threw such another stone at his mistress, up to the top of a hill, at a small distance; and that she in return, threw this mass down to him. It was all in sport.' Johnson, who generally pre-ferred fact to fiction, was puzzled, but he accepted that the stones 'were never put in their place by human strength or skill.' An earthquake was the probable cause. Yet this unnatural phenomenon which seems to con-tradict the laws of gravity cannot but suggest a supernatural agent and, as Johnson says, 'All nations have a tradition, that their earlier ancestors were giants.' Others have regarded the Coll stones as sacred, and believe they mark the site of Druidic worship.

Tiree, too, has its uplands – towards the

south-western tip of the island Ben Hynish, the tallest hill, reaches 460 feet and another Ben Hough, with a slight difference in spelling from Coll's is just under 400 feet. It overlooks a large bay to which it gives its name. And by a curious coincidence, Tiree also has a notable boulder, known as the Ringing Stone. It is about five feet high, poised on smaller rocks in such a way as to leave a hollow underneath, rather as casters lift an armchair from the floor. When the main mass is struck, it rings out. The Ringing Stone stands by the shore, a mile or so east of Balephetrish Bay, up the coast from Ben Hough. There is a legend attached to it – they say that

the Ringing Stone holds Tiree's destiny
within its rough-hewn form, for should it
ever be shattered the island would sink into
the sea.

The many similarities between Coll and
Tiree, some obvious, others unexpected,
were regarded by Martin as heaven-sent. He
saw it as providential that Coll produced
more boys than girls and Tiree, the reverse,
'as if Nature intended both these Isles for
natural Alliances, without being at the trouble
of going to the adjacent Isles or Continent to
be matched'. Martin quotes the 'parish book'
of his day as the source of this unusual
statistic.

The story of how these 'alliances' were formed, and fought over, goes back a long way, to the early days when both islands were inhabited by the Picts – Tiree may well have been the first place in Scotland where this still mysterious people settled, possibly arriving there from Ireland. We know very little of their way of life, which remained largely unchanged until Columba and his disciples arrived in the sixth century to bring Christianity to the Hebrides. Columba's mission, which was part political, eventually led him as far north as Inverness to the court of the Pictish king Brude. But Iona remained the headquarters of the religious movement, and the neighbouring islands its immediate target. On Tiree, for instance, a daughter monastery was founded by Baithen, Columba's cousin and close friend, who succeeded him as Abbot of Iona.

The Celtic Church, which owed only a loose allegiance to Rome, was tolerant of local practices, many of which survived by taking on a Christian form. As with sacred springs and wells, so with festivals. Michaelmas, for instance, which was widely celebrated, remained until quite recently the most important day in the holy calendar. It was marked by a cavalcade and racing events in honour of St Michael in his role as patron of horsemen. This is a very different St Michael from the one who attended Columba as he lay dying, with clear affinities to the Sun God worshipped in pre-Christian times and some obvious links with the ancient pagan rites of

Hallowe'en. The monks, who founded their primitive monasteries on the islands, lived much the same simple life as the local people and may well have succeeded in introducing new agricultural techniques to the general benefit. At any rate, they seem to have been accepted by the Picts who were eventually absorbed. This once-powerful people, who occupied large tracts of the mainland as well as most of the islands, have left relatively few traces. On Tiree, a number of standing stones and stone circles may date back to their times; of the early forts, brochs and duns, the best preserved is Dun Mor Vaul on the north coast across the island from Gott Bay. It was excavated in the mid-sixties. The broch known as the Great Fort of Caolas nearby is badly eroded, but still worth a visit if only for the site and the views. A local guide book lists more than twenty duns on Tiree, three of them on the tiny offshore islands of Salum and Kenavara. They are in various states of preservation – time and weather have done their destructive work; so has man's greed and indifference. Ceann a'Baigh, for instance, an inland dun which may once have served as the island's arsenal, was quarried last century to provide the stone which went to build a dyke at Crossapol. Coll has eight duns on record. The chief one is Dun an Achaidh, near the hamlet from which it takes its name, and further along the moorland road to Totronald, there are two standing stones six foot high. All that remains of the two islands' early inhabitants, mainly the ruins of fortified places, bears mute testimony to the long centuries during which they lived under the constant threat of violence – of raids on their cattle, the looting of their few goods, the sacking of their domiciles. The Christian church survived; its monuments did not. They too went down in a new wave of attacks from overseas. From the seventh century onwards, all religious settlements were prey to the Norsemen whose dreaded 'dragon' ships were never far from the coast. As a general rule, the monks who escaped the periodical massacres set about re-building with ant-like persistence, not only their cells of clay and wattle and thatch, but the stone churches. On Tiree, the monastery of Soroby was burnt down in 672, but a hundred years later it was still presided over by an abbot, who died in 774.

The Scandinavian bard, or skald, Bjorn Cripplehand, described the devastation. He speaks of the birds of prey gorged on human carcases, of the wolves with their jaws dripping blood which descended on 'Tiree's lonely shore'. Up to a point, plundering ceased once the Vikings decided to colonise the smaller islands, but internecine warfare continued between the various Norse rulers, whether converted to Christianity or not. By then, Church property was hardly more than a memory retained in the many place names which start in 'kil' – the Gaelic word for a church or chapel. Among the sand dunes at Kilkenneth on Tiree, there are the remains of an ancient chapel named after the Irish saint who was a contemporary of Columba's; another at Kenavara is dedicated to Saint Patrick and is judged to belong to early Christian times; at Kenovay, grass now covers the foundations of St Finan's chapel. Eleven ancient chapels are recorded on Coll, but some are hard to find and even more difficult to date. Searching for the past is a specialised occupation.

Under Norse rule, the official attitude towards the Church was ambivalent, typified by a tale told of Magnus Barelegs, the Norwegian king who is said to have earned his sobriquet by adopting Highland dress, the short kilt which uncovered the knees. By the end of the eleventh century the Western Isles had been ceded to him. The Sagas relate that during a tour of his newly acquired territories, the king anchored off Mull to visit Iona where he paid homage to St Columba by according 'quarter and peace to all men, and to the household of all men'. He then went off to plunder Islay.

The Western Isles returned to the Scottish crown under the Treaty of Perth, signed in 1266, three years after King Haakon's defeat at Largs. In the meantime, the powerful figure of Somerled came to dominate the scene. Born of a Celtic father, Gillebride of Clan Angus and a Norse mother, daughter of a king of Man, he gave neither side his allegiance and forged for himself a semi-autonomous Kingdom of the Isles, making peace with Olaf the Red, then king of Man, chasing his Norse kinfolk from the western seabord and most of the Hebrides and taking over Argyll to which his father had some genealogical claim. Contradicting his name which means 'the summer traveller', Somerled was the one who settled. Married to Olaf's daughter, Ragnild, he fathered the great clans: the MacDougalls, the MacDonalds and others who would continue to rule the Hebrides for several centuries until their power was finally broken with the Stewarts' defeat at Culloden. The islands Somerled took over had become divorced from the mainland – they were referred to as Innsegall or the Islands of the Foreigners. Now they were about to re-enter the mainstream.

The clans established a paternalistic rather than a strictly feudal system for their chiefs cared more for men than for money. Nevertheless, they arrogated to themselves all the powers once held by the great English barons and ruled with the right of life and death over their people, showing scant respect for the law of the land or the Crown. From them sprang the heroes who belong as much to legend as to history and whose names are common currency in the Hebrides. ClanDonald had Angus Og (the younger) who brought to Bannockburn at least a thousand men from the Isles (five thousand according to some accounts of the battle) and made certain of the Bruce's victory over the English. As a reward he was granted land in the Hebrides, including Coll and Tiree. Another important clan of this time the MacRuaris, also descended from Donald, Somerled's grandson, had not a hero, but a heroine. She was Christine MacRuari of Garmoran, head of the line in her own right, who sheltered and kept the Bruce hidden at her castle of Tioran in Moidart during the long months that he was on the run. The MacDonalds and the MacRuaris intermarried: Angus Og's son John taking Amy of Garmoran as his first wife and adding Eigg and Rhum to his other island possessions. He ended up ruling the entire Hebrides, both Inner and Outer. It was less than two centuries since Somerled (*d*. 1164) had brought unity and a measure of peace to the Western Isles, and now the balance of power had clearly swung in favour of the MacDonalds. The day of the MacDougalls, descended from Somerled's eldest son, was nearly over. Allied by blood to the Comyns, they found themselves on the wrong side during the Bruce's fight for Scotland's independence. They withdrew their allegiance and forfeited their lands following the murder of their kinsman, known as the Red Comyn. Suspected of betraying the Scottish cause to Edward the First, he was stabbed to death by the Bruce and his henchmen in a church in Dumfries where he had taken refuge. For this sacrilegious act, the Pope excommunicated the Bruce – to no great effect where the Scots were concerned. After his death, the MacDougall lands were returned to them and it seemed that reconciliation was complete when a MacDougall married one of the late king's granddaughters. Then fate took a hand – their son

John died without male issue and through his daughters, the Lorn inheritance passed into Stewart hands.

Scotland was now one country, united behind its borders. But the Hebrides remained remote, a kingdom in all but name where the MacDonalds and their vassals seemed all-powerful. A council of administration was set up; Dean Munro recorded that it consisted of fourteen members 'four of the greatest nobles, four thanes of lesser estate and four great men of the royal blood of Clan Donald' to which were added two ecclesiasts. Among the nobles – and most closely concerned with Coll and Tiree – were the Macleans of Duart and the Macleans (sometimes

Breachachadh castle

spelt MacLaine) of Loch Buie. The two branches of the clan, both centred in Mull, would continue feuding over land in the islands, but it was from one of the thanes on the council, MacNeil of Barra, that the Duart claimant would first wrest possession of Coll, and as Maclean of Coll, make Breachachadh his seat. Officially it is described (in a Scottish Tourist Board publication) as 'the best example of a fifteenth century West Coast castle'. But it is generally held that an older fort had preceded it on land granted by King Robert to Angus Og. As it now stands on the machair overlooking the waters of the bay, it consists of a square keep four storeys high whose mighty walls are seven feet thick and a circular tower, restored but in appearance much as it was when it came to the Macleans in 1431. Boswell was much interested in its name, 'Breachacha, or the Spotted Field, because in summer it is enamelled with clover and daisies, as Young Col told me.'

There are in fact two castles at Breacha-chadh, the old fortalice on the shore and above it on the hillside, the 'new' one, built in 1750 by Hector Maclean, Young Col's father. Boswell described it as a 'neat new-built gentleman's house' and he tells us that Dr. Johnson 'relished it much at first'. But Johnson got himself into trouble with posterity by complaining later that 'there was nothing becoming a Chief about it: it was a mere tradesman's box'. It is not indeed a castle, but a plain Georgian house whose proportions have been spoilt by the addition of meaningless turrets and crenellations. A sloping field separates it from the old fort providing rich grazing for rare breeds of sheep – four-horned Jacobs and Loghtans from the Isle of Man, Soays and Ronaldshays. The peaceful setting with its delicate colours is one of the most agreeable in the islands, but it must be said that the 'new castle' fits awkwardly into its surroundings.

The stormy weather which had driven Johnson and Boswell off course and forced them to seek refuge in Coll continued and for much of the time, rain kept them indoors. Johnson, always moody, soon became weary of their confinement. ('I want to be on the mainland, and go on with existence. This is a waste of life.') Boswell, however, kept himself happy rummaging among the old records he found in the house; there he came across the dramatic tale of how Ian Garbh and the Grizzled Lad had regained the island. 'Sturdy John' Maclean had been brought up in exile after his father died and his mother married MacNeil of Barra, who celebrated his nuptials by annexing Coll and settling there with his new wife. Grown to manhood, Sturdy John – the rightful owner as the islanders saw it – decided to reclaim his patrimony, which was now doubly threatened by the birth of a half-brother. Recruiting a force from Mull, he landed on Coll where the fighting soon became fast and furious and the Grizzled Lad was the hero of the day. Pitted against one of MacNeil's most powerful men, known as the Black Tailor, who was armed with a mighty battle-axe, he was driven back to the edge of a stream. Then the Lad seized the axe as he leapt back over the water, and hardly touching the far bank, forward again to behead his adversary with his own weapon. The battle field, near Grissipol, has entered the annals as Sloc na Dunaich, the Gully of Destruction. The Lad left to his chief the task of despatching both Macneil and his baby son. Another version of the story, however, has a happier ending – the child was spared and was eventually given Barra as his portion.

A landmark near Totronald known as Sruthan nan Ceann records another bloody encounter, this time between the Macleans of Mull and the Coll Macleans, which left the waters of the burn flowing red with decapitated heads, as the Gaelic name suggests. The feuding came about because of Lachlan Maclean of Duart's determination to involve the Coll Macleans in his many local disputes. They proved reluctant and, to force their hand, Lachlan mounted several punitive raids. When these failed, he decided to invade Coll. The day he chose was that of the old chief's funeral and the entire male population was following the body to the burial ground when the galleys from Mull were sighted. As one man, the procession turned to race down the hillside and overpower the force from Mull, which had counted on its taking some time for the men of Coll to muster. Those who landed were slaughtered, the rest sailed away. But they came back, and in the end Maclean of Duart occupied Breachachadh castle for several years till the Coll heir came of age and the Privy Council ruled that his lands should be returned to him.

Among the many tales that accumulated round the Macleans and their old castle, Dr Johnson selected the 'very memorable occasion' recalled by an inscription which 'not very long ago' he said, was to be seen engraved on the outer wall. The stone which bore it has long since disappeared, no-one knows how, where or when, but the events which led up to the treaty it recorded live on in history. The inscription read, 'If any man of the clan of Maclonich shall appear before this castle, though he come at midnight, with a man's head in his hand, he shall there find safety and protection against all but the king.'

The story starts with a grant of the lands of Lochiel made by James the Second to the Macleans. The lands, which had been forfeited, belonged to the Camerons and, as Johnson wrote, 'Forfeited estates were not in these days quietly resigned; Maclean, therefore, went with an armed force to seize his new possessions, and, I know not for what reason, took his wife with him. The Camerons rose in defence of their Chief and a battle was fought at the head of Loch Ness, near the place where Fort Augustus now stands, in which Lochiel obtained the victory, and Maclean, with his followers was defeated and destroyed. The lady fell into the hands of the conquerors, and being found pregnant was placed in the custody of Maclonich, one of a tribe or family branched from Cameron, with orders, if she brought a boy to destroy him, if a girl to spare her. Maclonich's wife, who was with child likewise, had a girl about the same time at which Lady Maclean brought a boy, and Maclonich, with more generosity to his captive, than fidelity to his trust, contrived that the children should be changed. Maclean being thus preserved from death, in time recovered his original patrimony; and in gratitude to his friend, made his castle a place of refuge to any of the clan that should think himself in danger.'

Dr Johnson says truly, 'This story, like other traditions of the Highlands, is variously related', but the main facts are established, and the practice of granting sanctuary in recognition of services rendered seems to have been common enough to judge by the example that comes from Tiree.

This story concerns the eleventh Maclean chief, that Lachlan who tried to drown his first wife, Lady Elizabeth Campbell, sister to the Earl of Argyll, during the dramatic episode recalled by the Lady's Rock in the Sound of Mull. Some say he tried to get rid of her because she failed to provide him with an heir; her successor, another Campbell surprisingly enough, also proved barren. At his third attempt, Lachlan turned to his own kin, a Maclean of Treshnish, and took her to live at Island House on Tiree where two sons were born. But soon she lost her heart to a handsome Irishman, William O'Buie. Their correspondence was intercepted by Lachlan, and since she did not deny her guilt, he planned a bloody revenge. He called on a local family, the Fionns, consisting of a father and seven sons, to go to Ireland and kill O'Buie; within a few days they were back to deliver his severed head to Island House. They were rewarded with a promise of immunity and soon put it to the test. One winter's night, the miller who also controlled the only crossing over the river retired early pulling up the drawbridge, with the result that one of the Fionn's horses returning from the moor with a load of peat lost its footing in the dark and drowned in the river. The Fionns retaliated by hanging the miller – a crime for which they were never punished. The story is still told round the fireside, along with the tale of Lachlan's end. He was murdered in Edinburgh in 1527, stabbed to death in his bed by a Campbell who broke into his chamber to deal out the long-postponed punishment Lachlan had earned by his attempt on the Lady Elizabeth's life. Eventually, the Island House passed into Argyll hands, though the present Victorian structure has little to do even with the house the Duke put up for his factor in 1748. That replaced an ancient fortress dating back to the first half of the fourteenth century, and perhaps earlier, which stood on an islet in Loch nan Eilean, reached by a causeway and a drawbridge. Even the site has changed for the channel which separated the castle from land was filled in long ago.

IV

Roads to The Isles (2) – North to Mallaig

Argyll influence spread throughout the Inner Hebrides and after the two Risings became predominant, leaving the Campbells to deal with some of the worst times the islands had seen, the Clearances and the Potato Famine of the 1840s. But although land changed hands, the old links held fast: in Coll and Tiree, Mull and the Macleans are regarded to this day as part of the extended family. There is a regular traffic between the three islands on the Cal-Mac ferries which stop at Tobermory to land and disembark passengers, islanders as well as tourists, and Tobermory, as much as Oban, is a good starting point for these small islands. Of the two, Coll is easier of access for the boats coming into harbour at Arinagour on their way to Scarinish give day-trippers a good couple of hours to make a first acquaintance with the island, while those who go on to Tiree must stay there for a night or two or return without landing. During the season, there is an alternative route – starting from Mallaig past Eigg and Rhum and round Ardnamurchan Head. This is how Bowman and his friend, sailing from Mull, first saw the 'Small Isles', as they are sometimes, rather misleadingly, called.

Rhum was the first to appear, with 'the very sharp points of two high mountains, which are about 2,300 feet high. As we doubled the northern point of Mull and left the Sound, a fine expanse of ocean opened before us ... in the north, over the Point of Ardnamurchan, rose the fine conical hills of Rum, and the black ridge of Egg capped with a perpendicular basaltic rock called the Scuir of Egg, looking like an immense broad tower, while between them faint and blue in the distance, but far succeeding them in altitude and grandeur, rose the high and battered peaks of the Cuchullin hills in the isle of Sky, peering over each other like masses of clouds. After proceeding a little further, we saw Muck and Canna, two small and low islands lying at the feet of the elegant isle of Rum, the former nearer to us on the eastern, the latter beyond it on the western side.'

Travelling from Harris some twenty years earlier, James Hogg had been equally impressed. 'We continued to move slowly on, and got some striking views of Egg, which hath a very romantic appearance from some points, especially from the N.W.' Hogg was even more taken with the 'stupendous mountains of Coolan', which he says formed 'a scene of the wildest grandeur'. Approaching Rhum, the mood changed: he was amused by the antics of the whales playing in the entrance of the bay. Whale-spotting in these waters remains a popular pastime, with cash given for the best photographs of these elusive animals who rarely show more than a gleam of their dorsal fin.

Splendid   scenery   and   unexpected

encounters with the local fauna provided the lighter side of the very serious business of sailing the Minch and the Sea of the Hebrides. Hogg's letter (to Walter Scott) in which he gives his first impressions of the Small Isles also contains an account of the dangers and difficulties of the voyage. Off Rhum, where the whales played, they were fog-bound, and when the fog lifted, a storm got up. Hogg suggested taking refuge in the deep harbour of Canna, only a few miles off, but the boat-men were determined to hold a southerly course for the mainland. Then, 'the wind increased again to a gale; the sea grew rough, and the vessel rolled again'. Hogg was unaffected, but his fellow passengers suffered horribly from sea-sickness. 'The motion of the vessel had also by this time thrown Mr. J into a morbid lethargy; he still kept to his hammock, and puked at times so violently, that I thought his chest should have rent.' They lost their bearings, and it turned out that the crew were unacquainted with the local waters. They landed up, not on the Scottish coast, but in the main harbour of North Uist, where Hogg, who was in no condition to do justice to Lochmaddy, dec-reed that 'it is not easy to conceive a more dreary and dismal-looking scene'.

It was fog over Rhum as well as the storm which drove Hogg's boat off course; similar conditions prevailed in 1844, when the influential evangelical writer Hugh Miller de-scribed the full fury of the weather that met the *Betsey*, a superannuated yacht chartered by the Free Church which he had joined on its mission to the Small Isles. 'The gale, thickened with rain, came down, shrieking like a maniac from off the peaked hills of Mull, striking away the tops of the long ridgy billows that had risen in the calm to indicate its approach, and then carrying them in sheets of spray about the furrowed surface like snow-drift hurried across a frozen field. But the *Betsey*, with her storm-jib set, and her mainsail reefed to the cross, kept her weather bow bravely to the blast, and gained on it with every tack. She had been a pleasure yacht, in her day ... who had used to encounter the swell of the Bay of Biscay.' The *Betsey* won through and at five o'clock in the morning dropped anchor in Rhum. There are still plenty of people who love sailing and all it entails to face the sea-trip to the Small Isles, but travelling most of the way by land became an easier, and faster, alternative for the less adventurous with the construction of the West Highland Railway. It was opened in August 1894 when it carried passengers as far as Fort William, and in 1901, it was extended to Mallaig.

The powers that be have set the west end of the Highland Line at Dumbarton, but there is all the difference between the southern and northern uplands. Travellers on their first journey north from Glasgow are introduced to the Highlands as the train runs along Loch Lomond. There is no doubt about the beauty of its 'bonnie, bonnie banks', as a homesick Jacobite called them, and few will disagree

61

with the many verdicts in its favour. To take but one – Nathaniel Hawthorne, the novelist who served as American consul in Liverpool in the first half of the nineteenth century, said the scenery was the loveliest he had ever seen. Other tributes came from the Continent, from a near contemporary, the influential German poet and novelist, Theodor Fontane, author of 'Beyond the Tweed', who called Loch Lomond 'a beautiful, noble stretch of water' fit to be known as 'the King of lakes'. The eighteenth century French geologist, Barthélemy Faujas de Saint Fond, describing the loch as 'superb', praised it in some detail: 'The fine sunlight that gilded its waters, the silvery rocks that skirted its shores, the flowery and verdant mosses, the black oxen, the white sheep, the shepherds beneath the pines.' Its beauties are indeed as delicate as they are changeable, varying with the season; green in spring when the long narrow lake and its many islands – there are more than thirty – are veiled by the fine tracery of budding larch and birch; in summer, when the far bank is golden with gorse and later in the year, rusty with bracken. Above the lake, cloud shadows play on the rounded summits of the mountains, Ben Lomond and its neighbours, Ben Vorlich and Ben a Chroin. Saint Fond especially liked Tarbet, where he stopped to take tea. 'I shall often dream of Tarbet', he wrote, 'even in the midst of lovely Italy, with its oranges, its myrtles, its laurels, and its jessamines.' The train leaves the loch at Ardlui, a pretty sight with pleasure craft swinging at their moorings, shortly to reach Crianlarich where the scenery changes to a wilder, and sometimes desolate grandeur. This is the very heart of the Highlands with the Grampian range stretching ahead, its high mountains blocking out the horizon over empty tracts of moorland and hardly a habitation in sight. The little station, its size bearing no relation to its importance as a main junction, remains a small community of no more than two hundred inhabitants whose grandparents came here to help build the railway. Crianlarich has stood at the cross-roads of history since it was a Roman outpost. It became a centre of Christianity in the seventh century when St Fillan arrived from Iona. He built a chapel in the vicinity (at Strath Fillan) and consecrated a local spring which had the unique quality of curing the insane. St Fillan's chapel crumbled, but was rebuilt by Robert the Bruce as a gesture of thanksgiving for his victory at Bannockburn. Again it fell into ruin, but Crianlarich carried on as a staging-post and today it stands at the half-way point of the West Highland Way, the hundred mile (or nearly) footpath opened in 1980 which runs from the outskirts of Glasgow to Fort William. In season, it is crowded with hill-walkers and the still more ambitious mountaineers setting out to climb some of the highest 'Munros' in the county, most of them nearer 4,000 feet than 3,000 – Ben More with its twin peaks, Stobinian, the heights of Glen Falloch and Ben Lui, where the river Tay has its source. A little further north stands the

Black Mountain where the Welsh naturalist Thomas Pennant made a note of an inn maintained by the government. 'Reach the King's house', he wrote, 'seated in a plain: it was built for the accommodation of his Majesty's troops, in their march through this desolate country.' Later, Kinghouse Inn was visited by the Wordsworths who thought little of its amenities, 'a miserable, wretched place', Dorothy called it. Pennant also stopped at Tyndrum, 'the small village' where yet another inn caught his attention since, 'it is seated the highest of any house in Scotland', a curiosity which he thought worthy of a special note in the index of his 'Tour' of 1769. Tyndrum is the next station after Crianlarich, which Thomas Thornton, a wealthy and eccentric sportsman, visited in 1804. He arrived with his party from the south, sorry to leave behind Loch Lomond, 'our delightful companion', to dine at the inn, or rather attempt to dine, as he put it. A rich man, accustomed to the best tables, he nevertheless admitted that 'uncomfortable as the house was, we found good eggs, fresh barley bannocks, and tolerable porter, together with some smoked salmon' – which might strike the modern tourist as something of an unexpected feast. Apart from shooting, food and fishing were Thornton's main hobbies, and reinforced with 'some good brandy and water' he was well pleased with the time he spent on the river Dochart. It had been an average day, for there is nothing new in travellers criticising their accommodation nor in anglers satisfied with their catch, imaginary or not. In fact, the most startling thing in Thornton's diary entry for July 4th is his extraordinary spelling of Crianlarich, which he puts down as Cree in La Roche. He was a francophile, who owned an estate in France, but that is hardly enough to explain, or excuse, such an orthographic irregularity, which has puzzled more than one of his diaries' editors.

Thornton rode on, taking in more bad lodgings and more good fishing on his way east; modern anglers will be tempted to carry on north to Bridge of Orchy famous for its salmon pools, and for mere sightseers, its old stone bridge humped over the river, 'soo-backit' in the vernacular. James Hogg, making his way to Fort William, describes the river, 'the Orchy is a large river and there are some striking cascades in it. The glen spreads out to a fine valley on the lower parts, the soil on the river banks being deep ... As you ascend the river the banks grow more and more narrow, till at last they terminate in heather and rocks. Besides one of the cascades which I sat down to contemplate, I fell into a long and profound sleep.' The Orchy runs south of Rannoch Moor; to the north the Corrour stop is said to be the most remote station in the British Isles. Between the two, the moor lies, twenty miles or so by twenty of waste land, a chilling landscape of trackless bog a thousand feet above sea level. In Hogg's words, 'Tis indeed a most dreary region, with not one cheery prospect whereto to turn the eye. On the right hand lies a prodigious

65

extent of flat barren muirs, interspersed with marshes and stagnant pools; and on the left, black rugged mountains tower to a great height, all interlined with huge wreaths of snow.' The opinion of the few travellers who attempted this stretch of the country, in his day and before, is unanimous – barren, desolate, gaunt, savage are the adjectives most commonly used. This was terra incognita, neglected and unknown by southerners. Daniel Defoe was one of the first to venture, and he thought little of it. To him the whole region was 'barren and pitiful'. He described the Lochaber district as 'indeed a frightful country . . . full of hideous desart mountains

and unsurpassable, except to the Highlanders who possess the passes.' Forty years later, Pennant continued to ignore the scenery: all he had to say of Loch Aber itself was that it was 'a lake not far from Fort William' and that Banquo had been murdered on its shores. There was, however, one redeeming feature – the trees. Loch Rannoch, for instance, was recommended to the Wordsworths as being 'bedded in a forest of Scottish pine'. And though he belonged to an age which did not regard the beauties of nature as worthy of much notice, even Pennant had something to say in its favour. 'Part of the southern (bank) finely covered with a forest of pine and birch, the first natural woods I had seen of pine: rode a good way into it . . . the ground beneath the trees is covered with heath, bilberries and dwarf arbutus, whose glossy leaves make a pretty appearance.' In modern times, Dr T. Radcliffe Barnett, a man who came to know the district well as he tramped the Highlands between the two World Wars, wrote of the great trees that are its glory. 'They are all ancient Scots pines, all of them being self-seeded. Is there anything finer in nature than a great pine tree – tall, rugged, strong and majestic, standing for centuries and defying the storm which roars hoarsely through its branches?' Loch Rannoch is at the very centre of Scotland, halfway between Ardnamurchan and Fife, equidistant from Inverness and Glasgow and its Black Wood was once no more than a small part of the great Caledonian Forest which covered the Highlands. There is very little of it left now, damaged by deer but ravaged by man, with his demands for timber and industrial fuel. From the seventeenth century onwards, ironworks used wood for smelting with the result that nearly two hundred years ago, Hogg was writing that the natural firs he had admired were but 'a poor remembrance of the extensive woods with which (the) environs have once been over-run'. The forest had covered even the stony wastes of Rannoch Moor, as the engineers discovered when they were laying the railway track. How the work was carried out is the moor's success story, and it is worth telling in a contemporary version. 'As it was impossible to get a solid foundation for the line on the bogland, the engineer, the late Mr Charles Forman, cut deep longitudinal and cross drains, laid layers of brushwood on the drier surface, and on this floating raft set the ballast, sleepers and rails, the peaty water actually preventing the decay of the wood.' And as this feat of engineering progressed, there appeared the massive tree roots of the ancient forest.

Travelling on through 'the seven bens, the seven glens and the seven mountain moors', as the old song has it, the train soon reaches Fort William, which stretches along Loch Linnhe under the towering mass of Ben Nevis. With its grey granite houses on steep Cow Hill overhanging the busy main street and the long neat promenade along the water, with its Episcopalian church and local museum, it seems a very Scottish town. Yet it has a special connection with the English since it was built up as a military outpost in Oliver Cromwell's time. Then it became Maryburgh, named after William the Third's Queen, and finally Fort William, following Mary's death. Situated at the west end of the Great Glen, it completed a chain of command which eventually stretched via Fort Augustus to Inverness in the east. A man who knew it well in the 1720s was Edward (possibly Edmund) Burt, an English officer stationed there in General Wade's day as 'Chief surveyor during the making of roads through the Highlands,' according to the notice which appeared in the Scots Magazine when Burt died in 1755. The notice also mentioned this soldier-cum-journalist's best-known publication 'Letters from a Gentleman in the North of Scotland', in one of which he describes Fort William. 'The fort is situated in Lochaber, a country which, though bordering upon the western ocean, yet is within the shire of Inverness. Oliver Cromwell made there a settlement . . . but the present citadel was built in the reign of King William and Queen Mary, and called after the name of the king. It was in great measure originally designed as a check upon the chief of the Camerons, a clan which in those days was greatly addicted to plunder, and strongly inclined to rebellion . . . the town was originally designed as a sutlery to the garrison in so barren a country, where little can be had for the support of the troops.' The old earthworks put up by General Monk in 1645 have gone; so has the stone fort which replaced them. They were pulled down to make place for the railway. Nor is there anything left of the town which, when Burt knew it, was built of timber, boards and turf – by special ordnance, he says, neither stone nor brick were to be used so that the houses 'might the more suddenly be burnt, or otherwise destroyed, by order of the governor, to prevent any lodgment of an enemy that might annoy the fort, in case of rebellion or invasion.' Fort William did in fact withstand a siege lasting five weeks during the '45, but with the final defeat of the Jacobite cause and the pacification of the Highlands, it seemed to have lost its purpose. As Bowman said, it had been developed to 'keep in check the restless spirit of the neighbouring chiefs, who adhered firmly to the cause of the Stuarts', and when he visited it at the end of July 1825, he found it 'gradually falling into ruins'. He was unduly pessimistic, however, for he ignored the lure of Ben Nevis, tallest mountain in Britain, which has ensured Fort William's future as a successful tourist centre.

Mountaineering as an organised activity is of fairly recent date, but the urge to conquer heights is as old as travelling man. Hogg, for instance, arrived footsore in Fort William after trudging more than twenty miles over the hills ('my feet were very much bruised'); yet after a night's rest he was writing 'I was uncommonly intent on being at the top of Ben Nevis, which is agreed by all to be the highest mountain in the British Islands, but the mist never left its top for two hours during my stay,' – an experience shared by many modern visitors. Bowman was luckier: after a few days spent recovering from the fatigues of the journey, he found himself with Dovaston 'upon the extremest summit' of the Ben drinking whisky diluted with snow since the nearest well was two miles away. They had chosen an 'auspicious' day and from where they sat they would have seen across Scotland from the North Sea to the Atlantic, from the north-east to Colonsay in the south-west and some say the coast of Ireland itself. On an earlier expedition, again on a hot day, Bowman and Dovaston had taken in Inverlochy Castle, the stronghold which stood at the very top of Loch Linnhe where Loch Eil joins it at right angles. It is now a ruin and tourists visiting Inverlochy generally make for the granite building in Victorian style which houses one of Scotland's most luxurious hotels. But when Bowman saw the old castle, a four-square building with round towers at the corners, mighty walls nine feet thick and the remains of a drawbridge, it still had the appearance of a substantial fifteenth century fortress. It may have been built as early as the thirteenth century by Edward the First or his Scottish allies, the Commyns, who gave their name to one of the towers. And Bowman was told that it might be older still, dating back to the days when it was the seat of the thanes of Lochaber and Banquo's favourite walk in the castle grounds was called after him. From Inverlochy, Bowman and his friend got a good view of Ben Nevis and 'were perfectly astonished, while broiling under the beams of a burning sun in the Dog days, at seeing many large masses of snow lodged in the clefts and lying on the sides of this mountain'. They were lucky, for it is seldom that Ben Nevis, 'the mountain with its heads in the clouds' reveals itself so completely. One of the best spots from which to view it is Corpach which the two friends visited on the day of their successful climb. The history of Corpach is in its name which means 'the place of dead strangers'; as their guide told them, it had been the stop on the waterside from which 'their ancestors embarked the bodies of illustrious strangers on their way for interment on Iona', Corpach and the neighbouring village of Banavie, both modern now, introduce their visitors to what is perhaps the most famous stretch of the Caledonian Canal – it is here that the sixty mile artificial waterway reaches its triumphant conclusion in the series of eight lochs known as Neptune's Staircase which raises the level of the water by sixty-four feet. The Canal, which made use of Loch Lochy, Loch Oich and Loch Ness, was cut between 1807 and 1822 on plans drawn up by James Watt and supervised by Thomas Telford to do for shipping what General Wade's roads had done for the troops. The waterway, as well as the roads, follows the Great Glen, the natural corridor provided by a geological fault which slices through the Highlands. Its military importance had been recognised from the earliest times; now it has been taken over by tourism. But away from the crowds, canal life, with the slow emptying and filling of the lochs, continues along the towpaths, sailing boats slip quietly between the banks under the shade of ancient trees, and the sluice keeper's house which Telford built still stands.

The Canal travels east; the road to Mallaig lies to the west along the shores of Loch Eil which divides Moidart from the Morars, then north along the coast. This stretch of the journey offers yet another aspect of the Highlands, perhaps the most beautiful of all. High hills and mountains withdraw to make a backdrop against the eastern sky to a scene

Caledonian Canal

where land gives way to water. Lochs cut
deep inland from a series of peninsulas and,
from the Sound of Arisaig to the Sound of
Sleat, it becomes difficult to tell lake from sea.
The track winds past broad bays surmounted
by cliffs and crowded with islets and travels
on through forests of pine and graceful birch.
The light plays tricks with the clouds, chang-
ing their colour and shape till they seem like
land masses in reverse. This is wild country,
and remote, and the names of the small
stations along the way are as chapter headings
in the history of Bonnie Prince Charlie's great
adventure. His monument stands at Glenfin-
nan, erected in 1815 on the beach below the

viaduct. Queen Victoria, forgetful of her ancestry, declared that she had never seen 'a lovelier or more romantic spot.' A slender tower on which stands the figure of a High-lander – not as is often thought of the Prince himself – marks the spot where the crimson and white standard of the Stuarts was raised on 19th August 1745. The Marquis of Tulli-bardine took part in the ceremony. A veteran of the cause, attainted and exiled after the 1715 rising, he was one of the small suite that accompanied Charles Edward from France. Three anxious weeks and more had gone by since they landed, dropping anchor in Loch nan Uamh, during which the Prince attempted to rally his supporters. The news of his arrival had been received with mixed feelings – in the Highlands most wished him well and would have been glad to see the Scottish crown back where it belonged with the Stuarts. But the chances of placing it there seemed slim – there were many who thought the enterprise doomed, with few resources and little hope of success. Some refused the Prince's summons outright, at least until France had delivered the money and men she had promised. They included the two influential leaders, Sir Alexander MacDonald of Skye and from Dunvegan, the Macleod of Macleod. Others wavered. But a morning came when the pipes were heard over the hills heralding the arrival of the Camerons of Lochiel. With the MacDonalds of Morar and Keppoch, the Stewarts of Appin and many others, a force of some five thousand men was formed to march on Edinburgh

First came victories, then defeat. The great adventure which began at Loch nan Uamh ended there – a French armed brig, the *du Teillay* (Walter Scott names it the *Doutelle*) had brought the Prince in via South Uist; in the September of the following year, another French ship, by an unfortunate coincidence called *L'Heureux*, evading the English patrols, slipped into the loch to carry him away for good. The cause was lost, but the man-hunt had failed. The fugitive with a price of £30,000 on his head was shielded to the last by the Highlanders' sense of hospitality and honour.

Loch nan Uamh – between Arisaig and the small peninsula of Archnish which separates it from Loch Ailort – is not on the railway line; the next stop is Arisaig. But it is well worth a detour for its rocky coast, its shining shingle beaches patrolled by oyster-catchers as well as for its romantic memories, which include the Prince's Beach by the Borrodale burn where he first set foot on the Scottish mainland.

Arisaig itself, a small seabord village with a population of less than two hundred, is to my mind rather under-rated. It has a pleasant hotel, a short row of shops. a petrol station; the 'bus stops there on its daily journey from Mallaig to Fort William and back. It looks out over Loch nan Cilltean where many little islands have been taken over by seal colonies. There is no formal port or pier – you cross the road and make your own way down by beaten tracks to the moorings where a small ferry waits to run out to Eigg and Rhum and Muck, and sometimes to Skye. The surrounding country, secluded but accessible, is full of delightful surprises for the town-dweller – honeysuckle and herons, deer in

Curlew

woods of birch and rowan, water-lilies on the lochans, the lonely cry of the curlew and the rattle of the corncrake. The views out to sea reach over silver sands as far as the Cuillins of Skye; as night falls, the inshore skerries are outlined against the setting sun which lays down a golden path along the water for a charter boat setting off to carry late travellers home to Eigg after a day's shopping in Glasgow.

There is now only one more stop before journey's end – Morar, a mere three miles from Mallaig. It is another small village with fewer than three hundred souls, but unlike Arisaig, perched on the dunes above what are probably the most famous sands on the West Coast – an expanse of white gold along the shallow bay where the ebbing tide recedes practically out of sight. The river Morar issuing from the loch only a quarter of a mile inland cascades down towards the beach; the loch itself, more than a thousand feet deep, is the result of a still unexplained geographical freak. The south bank is virtually inaccessible; a road runs along the north side past a group of wooded islets as far as the hamlet of Bracora, then it turns into a track leading across a narrow isthmus to reach Loch Nevis and North Morar. The small islands behind Morar sheltered for a while one of the most controversial figures of the '45, Lord Lovat, known as the 'Old Fox'. Walter Scott wrote of him, 'no-one suspected Lovat of attachment to King or political party further than his own interest was concerned'. His attitude was not unusual though he took it to extremes and his story reveals something of the corridor politics which formed an unsavoury background to the Jacobite movement. Though it was his son who commanded the Fraser troops at Culloden, Lovat himself was executed, beheaded at the Tower along with his peers, the two Earls of Kilmarnock and Cromarty and Lord Balmerino; lesser mortals were hanged, drawn and quartered. Lovat's son was later pardoned.

It is in the hinterland, not in Mallaig itself, that Bonnie Prince Charlie is best remembered – at Borrodale House, in Cluny's cage, the hide-out of the wily chief of Clan MacPherson on the slopes of Ben Alder, among the glens and forests and trackless wastes of the surrounding countryside. The Prince did in fact sail into Mallaig after his famous adventures with Flora MacDonald who brought him safely through Skye. Taking off from Loch Eishort for the short crossing of the Sound of Sleat, he landed in July 1746 to find the redcoats encamped on the shores of Loch Nevis. Avoiding the town, he was then forced to spend several days and nights on the open moor. He lives on in memory with the thousands upon thousands of tourists, many of them from overseas, who make use of Mallaig's ferry service to pursue his romantic trail through Skye. But Mallaig remains what it always was – a busy port where tackle crowds the quays and in a good season, it is a wonder that the fishing boats achieve their moorings.

EIGG

BAY OF
LAIG

CLEADALE

LOCH NAM
BAN MÓRA

KILDONNAN

SCURR
1290'

CASTLE
ISLAND

CAVE OF
FRANCIS

GALMISDALE

EILEAN NAN EACH

SOUND
OF
EIGG

GALLANACH

PORT MOR

BEN
AIREIN

MUCK

0   3

MILES
APPROX

V

The Small Isles – Eigg, Rhum, Muck and Canna

It was raining hard when the train drew into the small station across the road from the pier and it continued to do so all night, the water rattling down noisy as pebbles on a tin roof. It ceased at dawn, to be replaced by thick fog. At the hotel on the hill, I had been given a nice table by the bay window which should have overlooked the harbour, but the black-out was complete. Then, as I finished my local kipper and poured out a second cup of coffee, a transformation scene took place – with startling speed, the curtain was lifted, roofs and pavements still wet from the night's soaking glittered in the sun, the water shone, the bay grew busy, and Skye appeared against the sky-line.

Skye, the biggest and to many the most beautiful of the Inner Hebrides, has different faces – from Mallaig it shows itself at its most smiling, a neat landscape of low hills and woods and good green moorland grazing stretching down to the shore, out to the Aird of Sleat. One can make out the tidy little township of Ardvasar and the fine plantations of the MacDonald estate, where once the old castle stood, and all through the day, watch the ferry on the half-hour crossing to the landing stage at Armadale and back. From Easter to autumn, the boats are crowded with

Mallaig Harbour

passengers eager to set foot on the 'Misty Isle', not misty on that day but now welcoming in sunshine. A fine day following a storm is nothing unusual in the Hebrides – nor unfortunately is the reverse. The immediate attractions of Skye need no gloss and seizing the chance to visit it from Mallaig, no excuse. The old route from Glenelg, which Dr Johnson took with Boswell, entails a hard drive through the great headland between Loch Hourn and Loch Duich; the shortest, possibly the most popular crossing from the Kyle of Lochalsh is much easier to reach from Inverness than by road across Knoidart. Because Skye is infinitely varied – even its mountain

ranges, the Cuillins and the Quiraing, are entirely different – it needs time to explore. So
there is something to be said for resisting the
temptation to sail off at once on a day trip and
instead, spending an hour or two taking Mallaig in before catching a ferry to the 'Small
Isles'.

Mallaig is seldom starred in the guide
books; some, indeed, treat it as a mere rail-
head. Nor has it the metropolitan flavour of
Fort William or Oban, with their many shopping opportunities. In a way, it is a survival, a
typical West Coast fishing port whose fortunes have depended on the catch. The hub of
the town is the port at the south end of the

bay; a road well worth taking leaves the centre to follow the shore's curve under whitewashed houses scattered over the moorland slopes overlooking the anchorage. Tourists are well catered for, but one gets the impression that the fishing fleet matters more. Herring and crustaceans are the main concern; where deep-sea fishing is concerned, Mallaig has shared the fate of other West Coast ports, which, starved of resources, lost out to the East Coast where the new steam-boats were being built. Sail could not compete. But the herring still arrive though the boats that land them may come from afar as they chase the shoals in their yearly migration round Scotland. They are eagerly awaited by a bustle of packers and loaders and lorry-drivers joined by sightseers and other idlers – and by the gulls. As the holds are emptied, the gulls scream and fight for the fish that fall out, sometimes catching them in mid-air, and attack the decks for those that slither out of the nets. A small industry has grown up, smoking, salting, kippering, freezing, with sheds selling local produce on the quayside. Fish-farming has now taken hold, specialising in lobster and prawns which continue to make their contribution to the economy. All the way from Arisaig to Mallaig, there still are nets drying on the shore and lobster creels clutter the piers, though the old 'pots' of wickerwork plaited on dark nights by the fireside have given way to more modern traps. The floats once made of blown-up sheepskins were replaced by glass long ago;

the nets themselves, which once incorporated horse-hair, have displaced the old baited line. Times change, though many complain that the government's neglect of the infrastructure in these parts does not. It is easy to recapture the past in Mallaig, and another journey into the old days awaits one in the islands out to sea as the ferry weighs anchor for Eigg and Muck and Rhum and Canna.

The puzzle about the Small Isles is that they are not especially so. Muck, a mere 2½ square miles is indeed no bigger than many of the islets in the Firth of Lorn or the Treshnish group, but Eigg, 8 miles long by 5 across, is much the same size as Colonsay and Rhum, the largest, measures about 8 miles each way; Canna is about 5 miles from east to west though hardly more than a mile from north to south. The appellation seems to belong to ecclesiastical history rather than to geography, to the post-Reformation days when a non-resident minister was appointed to officiate for the whole group. The first was Neil MacKinnon from Sleat in Skye who took up his duties such as he conceived them *circa* 1620. Until then and well into the eighteenth century, the islands were generally referred to, notably by Boswell, as the 'popish islands'; they became an official separate Protestant parish in 1727.

Of the four, the smallest, Muck, is the most fertile; Rhum with the formidable profile of its high peaks always on the skyline, is the most mountainous and barren; though its coast, all cliffs and caves and rocky outposts, makes Eigg difficult to approach, it has its stretches of moorland, its woods and beaches of shell-sand; Canna, away to the north, has rich soil naturally well drained. Martin had already recognised some of these merits, and, as was natural for an early mariner, had singled Canna out for the 'good Anchorage in the North-East'. Although it was 'for the most part surrounded with high Rock', Canna was 'fruitful in Corn and Grass', and the same went for low-lying Muck. The coastal reaches of Rhum qualified as 'arable and fruitful' and Martin noted its salmon rivers, and the hundred deer in its mountains. As to landing, he had an unexpected warning against the bay of Loch Scresort, generally considered a reasonably safe haven, the only one on the island. According to Martin, however, its east side 'is not fit for anchoring, except without the Entry'. Martin's report on Eigg is longer than most, covering several pages; it includes a lot of local folklore, as well as a description of the island's most famous feature, the Sgurr of Eigg. As to its agricultural potential, Martin estimated it as 'indifferent good for Pasturage and Cultivation'.

After rounding Ardnamurchan Head, travellers approaching Eigg from the south are treated to a magnificent panorama of islands, bounded in the north by the faint blue line of the Uists and Benbecula and soon dominated by Hallival and Askival and behind Rhum, by the Cuillins of Skye. Then appears the Sgurr, the imposing mass of columnar pitchstone which rises to more than twelve hundred feet over the southern end of Eigg. It is crowned by a three hundred feet block of black lava over-hanging the coastline which looks like an ancient fortress. In fact some early guide books suggest that there was once a fort on the site. The Sgurr, with two perpendicular faces dropping sheer away, is prolonged by a mile-long ridge which has been compared to Ireland's Giant Causeway; Noel Banks (*Six Inner Hebrides*) has described its surface as 'a cobbled street contorted by an earthquake', which does not make for easy walking. But the view makes it worth the effort – an empty countryside with small lonely lochs lying to the north and west. An islet on one of them, Loch nan Ban Mora, is said to have held a Viking settlement; the rest of the lochs are inhabited only by the Kelpie, the Highlanders' dreaded water-horse who lies in wait to lure, then drown, benighted travellers. It is a dark scene, of gleaming water and black stone. Coming from further north, on the regular ferry service from Mallaig, or as Neil Gunn did from Skye, sailing off in his boat from Loch Bracadale, the Sgurr is first seen rearing up at the end of the long stretch of east coast cliffs, which some say remind them of the Great Wall of China. They put me in mind of something equally exotic, at least as recalled from the Hebrides – the Colosseum at Rome. For the cliffs appear to be terraced and the sandstone of which they are composed has eroded into the shape of doors and arches and

windows. The last landmark was the Point of Sleat, where the white waves were foaming over the skerries; now the ferry was negotiating the tricky entry past Castle Island to the pier at Galmisdale, and during its manoeuvres, there was time to admire a very different landscape. South from the point of Kildonnan onwards, there are small bays and fine sands, and behind the harbour where we were now mooring, the brae is green and well-wooded, and the main road through the island leads up and off through the trees.

How the Sgurr of Eigg came into being has not yet been decided. According to some authorities, it is the sole remnant of a range of

pre-historic mountains rising from the valley of a river which originated in Wester Ross, or it might even be the Tweed itself. Others believe that a volcanic upheaval threw up the great hill as it laid low an ancient forest and base their argument on the discovery of fossilized trees. A mystery is also attached to the adjoining coast of cliffs and caves, but this one is a matter for historians, not geologists: what is the truth behind the Massacre of the Cave of Francis?

Martin is one of the first to mention the cave itself. In a short, and very accurate description of the southern aspect of Eigg, he writes: 'There is a Mountain in the South end, and on top of it there is a huge Rock call'd Skur Egg, about one-hundred-and-fifty paces in Circumference . . . there is a Harbour on the South East side of this Isle, which may be enter'd into by either side of the small Isle without it. There is a very big Cave on the South West side of this Isle, capable of containing several hundred of people.' Such is Uamh Fhraing where in the year 1577 the entire population of the island – three hundred and ninety-five people is one figure given – took refuge during a raid by the Macleods and were burnt to death. The whys and wherefores of the massacre are still in dispute. Boswell did not visit Eigg; but Young Col told him the story which he summarised in his Journal on which the 'Tour' was based: 'I regretted that we passed the island of Eigg, where there is a very large cave in which all the inhabitants were smoked to death by the Macleods. They had murdered some Macleods who were sailing near their coast. Macleod and a number of the clan came to revenge the murder. The people of Egg saw them coming, and all returned into this cave, which has a low and narrow entry, so that but one man can get into it at a time, but afterwards becomes lofty and spacious like a church. Macleod and his people landed, and could not find a soul. They might perhaps have gone away. But one of the Egg people, after waiting a long time in the cave, grew impatient and went out to see what had become of the enemy. Perceiving them not gone, he returned. There was deep snow on the ground, by which means he was tracked by the print of his feet. The Macleods came to the mouth of the cave. Nothing could be done in the way of fighting, because but one man at a time could either go out or in and would be killed directly. Macleod called in to them that if they would give up the murderer, he would be satisfied. This they refused to do. Upon which he ordered a quantity of peats to be laid in the mouth of the cave and to be set on fire, and thus the people of Egg, man, woman and child, were smoked to death.' Young Col himself had visited the cave and seen great quantities of bones: they were so arranged, men's bones and women's and the bones of small children, as to indicate where whole families had huddled together for protection as the smoke and flames poured in; as Dr Johnson put it in his account 'lying dead by families as they stood'. He also recorded the story briefly and evidently regarded it as no more than an incident showing 'the disorderly state of insular neighbourhood'. It has a number of variants, and according to some a bloody sequel when many years later, a party of MacDonald raiders descended on Skye and set fire to the church at Trumpan, burning the congregation to death. But there seems to be no doubt about the presence of human bones in the Cave of Francis – Walter Scott saw them there in 1814 and took some away. 'I brought off, in spite of the prejudices of our sailors, a skull from among the numerous specimens of mortality which the cavern afforded.' To Dr Johnson, the massacre was no more than an incident typical of the times; to Walter Scott, it was 'a dreadful work of indiscriminate vengeance'. His account, in 'Tales of a Grandfather', is the most complete as well as the most dramatic. It suggests a motive for the islander's original maltreatment of the Macleods: 'About the end of the sixteenth century, a boat, manned by one or two of the Macleods, landed in Eigg . . . They were are first hospitably received; but having been guilty of some incivility to the young women on the island, it was so much resented by the inhabitants, that they tied the Macleods hand and foot, and putting them aboard their own boat, towed it to sea, and set it adrift, leaving the wretched men, bound as they were, to perish by famine, or by the winds and waves, as chance should determine. But fate so ordered it, that a boat belonging to the Laird of Macleod fell in with that which had the captives on board, and brought them to safety to the laird's castle of Dunvegan in Skye.' According to yet other accounts, the Macleod himself was among the party which first landed in Eigg. Some say they were driven there by a storm and were ill-received owing to the long-standing feud between the Macleods and the MacDonalds. Or that Macleod joined in molesting the women and was so badly beaten as a result that his back was broken and he remained a cripple. However that may be, one must wonder that the Macleods, returning on their punitive expedition, should have given the entire population of Eigg time to hide in a cave. Another complication arises: in 1588, after the defeat of the Armada, Maclean of Duart, pursuing a hereditary claim to the Small Isles, landed on Eigg with a force of armed men, including a hundred Spaniards from the *Florida*, the ship that had sought refuge in Tobermory and was subsequently blown up in mysterious circumstances. Maclean and his men are reported to have devastated the island and slaughtered its inhabitants – by burning them to death. Maclean was indicted for this offence and spent some time imprisoned in Edinburgh Castle. Two similar massacres in hardly more than ten years seem excessive.

The skeletons were removed from the cave in Victorian times, and Hugh Miller was one of the last visitors to see them there. Miller, who took time off from his missionary activities to explore the island, came across another of its puzzles – the Singing (or Sounding) Sands at Camas Sgiotaig, just north of Laig Bay up on the west coast. He tells us that walking across them with his companions, they 'performed a concert', the sound being 'a shrill sonorous note'. It has also been compared to the music of an Aeolian harp. The phenomenon is unusual, though not unique for there are similar sands elsewhere in Scotland as well as in the north of England and in the Channel Islands. The 'singing' effect is the result of air expelled under pressure between the tightly packed layers of tiny grains of sand, all of a size, which start rolling under the foot. But not when it rains, and Neil

Gunn exploring the Cleadale district as Hugh Miller had done was prevented from experiencing the Singing Sands. However, he got to know the beaches of Laig Bay which he describes as a 'smooth wide sickle of brown sand, where, in the soft sandstone, hard polished boulders are stuck like plums in the face of a cake.' The cliffs that line the coast, of sandstone and limestone, are so unstable that over the ages huge blocks have fallen away, leaving an intricate network of passages, ledges, hollowed-out caves, streams, rock-pools and waterfalls. Inshore, the land is fertile, good crop-growing country when there were crofters to work it. But some moved away and others were displaced to make room for the game demanded by the shooting estates, and the neighbourhood is now deserted. It is peopled only by memories of the giants who lived in the cliffs and tumbled them about and of the ghostly washerwoman who spends her time by the river laundering the shrouds of travellers who venture to ford it. But the uncommon Grass of Parnassus – a kind of white buttercup which smells of honey – flourishes on the rock-face, there are

Manx Shearwater

sea anemones in the pools, Manx Shearwaters fly over across the Sound which separates Eigg from Rhum. From the cliff top, a magnificent seascape spreads out; Hugh Miller saw it from still higher up, from the summit of the Sgurr and he wrote of the prospect of islands from 'Skye to Uist and Barra, and from Uist and Barra to Tiree and Mull. The contiguous Small Isles, Muck and Rhum, lay moored immediately beside us like vessels of the same convoy that in some secure roadstead drop anchor within hail of each other.'

Before setting off north to Rhum, there is time enough for a detour south to spend an hour to two on Muck, the small island without much history where there is little to do except enjoy it. Three miles from Eigg, it is about $2\frac{1}{2}$ miles square, its coast deeply indented especially on the north-west side where rocky headlands, like well-sharpened pencils, thrust out to sea. Dykes join Muck to its two outliers, the Isle of Horses and tiny Eagamol. At its western end, its single hill, Ben Airein rises to 450 feet. The harbour, Port Mor, stands at the head of a deep triangular bay, guarded – and hampered – by two practically parallel skerries which come near to closing the entrance. As a result, the ferry stands off till passengers wanting to land are taken off. This is the time to remember Neil Gunn's advice, 'Stepping into a dinghy is a simple enough matter, if done with decision; but to put one foot out and then hesitate is to ask for close communion with the sea.' The jetty at Port Mor is still a'building; for the

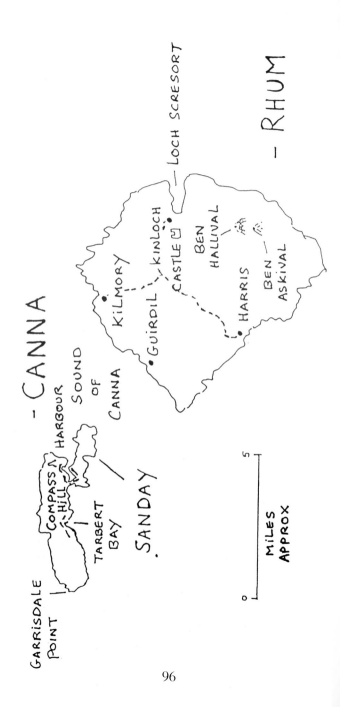

time being, access to Muck is up the steep stone steps cut into the harbour wall. But there are plenty of friendly hands to help the less agile and before long, one is on the road, the only one on the island, which crosses it to the north-west coast before taking a dog's leg turn on to the 'town' of Gallanach. Leaving behind the white-washed cottages of Port Mor, it is pleasant walking in the soft air along the unsurfaced road which brings back memories of country lanes, between open green fields some of them knee-deep in wild flowers. For company, there are the sheep, the cattle and long-haired goats. No cars are allowed on the island, apart from the odd Land Rover, shipped in specially from Fort William or even Glasgow, to meet the needs of local farmers and an old-fashioned tractor may come rumbling down the road. Children on their bikes greet you with innate Highland courtesy. Past pleasant coppices – Muck is too exposed to allow for serious timber – the road reaches low cliffs with a great open view north to Rhum and beyond and south to Ard-namurchan, about 8 miles away. Then it turns off to end at Gallanach, with its fine old farmhouse and walled garden. A mild climate and favourable soil have combined to bring a measure of prosperity to the island. In the eighteenth century, it was able to support one hundred and sixty souls, who paid their dues in 'exported corn'; two hundred years later it was early potato crops that helped meet the bills. Nevertheless, Muck has suffered de-population, as have its neighbours – by the end of the 1970s only a couple of dozen people were recorded as living there.

The happiest nations, they say, are those which have no history, and compared with other islands with their sorry tale of massacres and all the other cruelties of clan warfare, history seems to have passed Muck by. When it did enter the annals it was because of a celebrated dispute over its name. Muck in English signifies rubbish of an unpleasant nature; in Gaelic, it means 'pig'. As Dr Johnson noted, 'It is usual to call gentlemen in Scotland by the name of their possessions, as Raasay, Bernera, Loch Buy, a practice necessary in a country inhabited by clans, where all that live in the same territory have one name.' Now Muck's young laird seems to have been a model landlord – he would bring in a smith from Eigg and, no less than six times a year, a tailor from the mainland. Above all, he went to the considerable expense of two shillings and sixpence a head to have eighty of his people inoculated against the smallpox. But he had his pride and deeply objected to being referred to as 'Muck', 'thinking it too coarse for his island'. He put up a spirited campaign to have the name changed to Monk, arguing that this was its proper appellation since it had once been owned by Iona and a hermit had lived there. His claim fell on deaf ears, but a polite compromise was reached: he was henceforth addressed as 'Isle of Muck'. As to whether there ever was a holy man on the island, or swine – that is another matter. It has been said that Muck got its name from the porpoises, or sea-pigs, which frequent its coasts.

Names and their spellings, as well as their interpretation, are a feature of the islands, and Neil Gunn, a dab hand at producing their variants. For Eigg, as it is now generally spelled, he produces the following: Egga, Ego, Egea, Eiggie, Ardegga. Johnson and Boswell knew it as Egg. An unresolved philological dispute surrounds Rhum – or should it be Rum? It has been suggested, rather improbably, that the name with its Greek root referred to the island's shape, a parallelogram such as the ace of diamonds in a pack of playing cards. Dean Munro called it Ronin, which may or may not be derived from the Norse word for spacious or roomy. Rhum certainly has many place names ending in 'val' or 'dil', Norse words for hill and valley; yet there are no traces of Viking settlements on the island. Then again, why was the

Rhum landscape

spelling changed from Rum to Rhum? Was this a concession to Victorian proprieties in the days when neither sex nor spirits were mentioned in polite society? And was the rather silly little joke that dubbed Rhum and its neighbours the 'Cocktail Islands', with Canna standing for the raw sugar used in the cobblers and juleps fashionable in the Twenties, a reaction from Victorian repressiveness? About the only thing that purists at least agree on is that Rhum should be pronounced 'room' – which it seldom is. But there are better things to do than speculate about this strange island's name.

Rhum stands out from its companions in more ways than one – it rears over the sea, mountainous, wet, barren and inhospitable. Its one harbour at Loch Scresort is generally acknowledged to be difficult of access – Neil Gunn attempting it from Eigg failed to make it as the fog descended; in 1772 Pennant sailing south from Canna in 'a favourable gale in a rolling sea' managed to drop anchor in 'an open bay, about two miles deep ... called Loch Sgriosaig, bounded by high mountains, black and barren. The island is one great mountain', he wrote, and found 'on the South West side, precipices of stupendous height.' Pennant noted that there was very little arable land, but that the corn and potatoes it produced were very good. Villages and fields were concentrated along the coast at the seaward end of the four valleys which radiated from the centre – on the sandy bay of Kilmorin in the north, at Harris in the south-west, due west at Guirdil and in the east at Kinloch, where the island's small population (*circa* forty) is now centred. The deserted villages are man-made, for although the mountainous nature of Rhum restricts cultivation enough was produced in Pennant's day to maintain fifty-nine families. Of these, all were Protestant, except one which remained Roman Catholic. At the time, Rhum belonged to the Macleans of Coll who had bought it from the Clanranalds, its previous owners. The Clanranalds remained Catholic but Rhum's new laird had turned Protestant though his sister remained a Papist. One Sunday, as she led the congregation to hear mass, Maclean barred the way. Raising his stick, he hit one of the would-be worshippers on the head, then drove the rest off to the kirk, which he saw to it they continued to attend. In reference no doubt to the colour of the cane he carried, this became known as the 'Yellow Stick Conversion'. In later years, the island's lairds were to be equally high-handed in preventing their people from attending Free Church services. These were often held in the open air, sometimes on the shore. Dissenting ministers were turned out from the churches where they had previously officiated, and local lairds made certain that no suitable alternative was offered. In 1843, when the *Betsey* dropped anchor two hundred yards outside Loch Scresort with the Free Church minister, John Swanson, aboard, Hugh Miller wrote that 'Bad as the morning was, we could see the people wending their way, in threes and fours, through the dark moor, to the place of worship . . . the appearance of the *Betsey* in the loch had been the gathering signal; and the Free Church islanders – then a fourth of the entire population – had all come out to meet their minister.' The founding of the Free Church belongs as much to political as to religious history: though it insisted on the grimmer aspects of Calvinism, including the strictest observance of the Sabbath, it came into being largely as a protest against the Clearances at the time when the majority of the established clergy did nothing to defend their parishioners for fear of losing their benefices, the manses and glebes they held from their patrons, the lairds. The Clearances have left their mark all over the islands, but none suffered more than Rhum whose people were dispossessed first to make room for sheep, then for deer. Shortly after the Napoleonic wars, the island was leased as a sheep run and all but fifty of its inhabitants were evicted, most of them making their way to Nova Scotia. One result was a labour shortage and a few families from Muck and Skye were allowed in to settle on land unfit for sheep. In the end, the whole experiment in sheep-farming failed, and its initiator was forced to emigrate. A worse fate now awaited Rhum – what was left of its people were 'cleared' to make room for deer when the Macleans sold it as a sporting estate. It had various owners, including the Conservative Prime Minister, Lord Salisbury; then came the Bulloughs, who made their money in the cotton trade and spent it on importing unwonted luxuries to Rhum. A castle was built at Kinloch – of pink stone quarried in Arran and shipped block by block from the Clyde; gardens were laid out, ornamental pools dug, rivers diverted to improve the fishing. During the season, huge house parties were given with all the lavishness and ostentation of the Edwardian heyday. There were deer on the hills and salmon in the streams, but although some local employment was created and there were kindly 'perks', the population continued to decline. With the boys and girls leaving for the mainland went the old way of crofting life. The Bulloughs have their mausoleum, in the style of a small Greek temple built by the shore at Harris; there is none to the vanished communities. Touring the Highlands in 1935, Edwin Muir wrote: 'This is a land whose main contemporary industry is the shooting down of wild creatures, not products of any kind but wholesale destruction. This state of things is not the fault of the Highlanders, but of the people who have bought this country and come to it chiefly to kill various forms of life.' In Rhum, at any rate, wild life has had its revenge for the island was taken over in 1957 by the Nature Conservancy Council. Casual tourists are not encouraged; mountaineers, ornithologists and other visitors with a purpose are allowed in by arrangement. With essential exceptions, there are no cars on the island. But there is a fine herd of Highland cattle and the famous ponies have been re-introduced, small but 'eminent for beauty . . .

of a shape uncommonly elegant.' In Dr John
son's day, a Rhum pony was expected to
fetch as much as a guinea and a half. Some say
the breed was introduced by the Vikings;
others, that it developed from Spanish horses
which survived from Armada ships wrecked
on the coast of Rhum. There are still wild
goats, with their spectacular horns, and for
bird-watchers, the colonies of Manx Shearwaters that burrow out their nests in the
mountain tops. The red deer are back, about
fifteen hundred of them competently culled
every year to provide venison. On the way
to Canna, passengers equipped with long-dis-
tance lenses photograph them from the deck,
crossing the high moorland in Indian file.

For centuries, Canna has been playing hide-and-seek with history, and with geography too. To start with Canna is two islands, not one, but not everyone bothers to mention Sanday, the two miles of crofting land which disguises the entry to the harbour. You will find it on Ordnance Survey maps, but not in the average guide book. As Pennant saw it, 'each shore appeared pleasing to humanity; verdant, and covered with hundreds of cattle: both sides gave a full account of plenty, for the verdure was mixed with very little rock, and scarcely any heath'. Sanday provides an attractive approach to Canna's 'snug' harbour which has been known to seafarers down the ages and continues to offer shelter to ships running from a storm. Fishing fleets from all over Europe and still further afield reach haven there – and record the name of their vessels, in an unusual form of graffiti, on the cliff face lining the port's eastern edge. It was known to Baltic traders in the eighteenth century and used as a staging-post by seamen from the Outer Hebrides, sailing or rowing to Glasgow from the Uists and Barra with their cargo of hides to exchange for such necessaries as sugar and salt. Conscientious as ever in his self-imposed task of charting sea-routes, Martin noted the 'good anchorage', but what interested him most was a strange phenomenon in the north of the island, where a high hill 'disorders the Needle of the Compass; I laid the Compass on the stony Ground near it and the Needle went often round with great Swiftness, and instead of setting towards the North, as usual, it settled here due East. The Stones in the Surface of the Earth are black, and the Rock below facing the Sea is red; some affirm that the Needle of a Ship's Compass, sailing by the Hill, is disorder'd by the force of the Magnet in this Rock: but of this I have no certainty.' In turn, Pennant recorded this distortion: 'The needle in the mariner's compass was discerned to vary a whole quarter; the North point standing due west: an irregularity probably owing to the nature of the rock, highly impregnated with iron.' Pennant was right, and there was no reason for Martin's uncertainties; the 'black stone' he observed was the explanation – basalt heavily impregnated with iron which acted as a powerful magnet. Compass Hill, as it is now known, provides tourists on Canna with fine views 'over the sea to Skye'.

Canna is by no means flat, and from another of its more accessible heights, Sron Ruail at the western end of the island, the panorama includes Heskeir (or Hysker), the island seven miles south on the way to Coll, which once played an important part in Canna's economy. Nowadays, it is occupied by lighthouse keepers who share it with seals, shell-fish, bees, butterflies and sea-birds. Not more than a hundred years ago it provided juicy pasturage for Canna cattle. Cattle, and sheep, are still reared on Canna: Highlands and cross-breds whose winter fodder is grown locally, flocks of Blackface and Cheviots on the moor. The countryside is quite varied – and there are sandy beaches near Canna House and at Tarbert Bay, but most of the coast is bounded by cliffs and clusters of skerries which provide breeding grounds for many birds, including the rare sea eagle now successfully re-introduced on Rhum.

Porpoises (Gaelic: Canna) frequent the shores in summer and according to some authorities, give the island its name. There is here more than enough to satisfy naturalists and, in so small a compass, a surprising number of ancient remains for those more interested in the past. We cannot tell whether the Vikings to whom Compass Hill must have been a well-known landmark as they sailed south on their raids, ever attempted to settle on Canna, but they picked out a spot on its northern coast for one of their splendid ship burials, when the high flames from the pyre rose over the waters into the night sky. The site, one of the best preserved in the Hebrides, is at Rubha Langan-Innis, looking out to South Uist. Nor do we know in any detail what damage was done during the several centuries when the Norsemen, as well as freelance pirates, roamed the seas. All that is left are ruins, fragments of a disjointed past. What clues there are could be interpreted *in situ* – with the help of the local scholar, Dr John Lorne Campbell, who settled in Canna in 1938. Canna House shelters the library of Hebridean lore – Gaelic, Celtic, Scottish – which he and his wife (Margaret Fay Shaw) have built up over the years. Canna also owes some of its woodland to Dr Lorne Campbell, and native fishermen will not forget him as the co-founder (with the late author, Compton Mackenzie) of the Sea League to defend their right to the catch in local waters.

Even without scholarly guidance there is much to admire and enjoy in the duns and forts scattered about – in one of them a jealous laird is said to have imprisoned his beautiful young wife. Standing stones abound. A magnificent Celtic cross bridges the gap with pre-Christian times. Richly carved, in shape rather like an up-ended hammer, it stands by the chapel named after St Columba. Martin knew it when it still served its congregation: 'The Church of this Isles is dedicated to St Columba', he says. But whether Columba or any of his immediate followers came to

Canna is another matter. There are legends in plenty, factual evidence is more elusive.

So far from the mainland, the Hebrides were spared many of the excesses of what could well be called Scotland's Wars of Religion. Canna, along with Muck, had belonged to Iona – 'it pertains to the Abbot of Colmkill', as Dean Munro put it, then to the Clanranalds, and a strong Roman Catholic tradition had taken root. Pennant found that of the island's two hundred and twenty souls 'all except four families are Roman Catholics', the Reformation notwithstanding. Both cults were catered for, at least on paper.'The minister and popish priest reside in Eigg, but by reason of the turbulent seas, are very seldom able to attend their flocks.' As he was writing, Canna was still owned by 'Mr. Macdonald of Clan-Ronald', as he mis-pelled it. Later the island changed hands, belonging to the MacNeills, also Roman Catholics, who built Canna House *circa* 1820; now it is under the aegis of the National Trust for Scotland. The Roman Catholic church, erected in the 1890s by the Marquis of Bute, is now disused – it stands on Sanday at the end of the road which leads on from the old foot-bridge. Yet Canna is reluctant to let go of the old ways: it was the last of the islands to hold the Michaelmas cavalcade according to the ancient rite, with the great oatcake called Struan Michael baked for the occasion. Columba, prince, priest and politician, would not have objected.

COLONSAY

0   3

MILES
APPROX

KILORAN
BAY

BALNAHARD

LOCH AN
SCOLTAIRE

COLONSAY
HOUSE

PORT
OLMSA

KILCHATTAN   LOCH
FADDA

SCALASAIG

MACHRINS

GARVARD

THE STRAND

PRIORY

EILEAN
NAN
RON

ORONSAY

110

VI

Out to Sea – Colonsay and Oronsay

There is so much we are told about Columba and so little we know. There are innumerable questions, with few solid facts among an infinity of surmises. The one thing we do know for certain is that he settled on Iona and turned it into the sacred isle which took his name – Icolmkill. But his itinerary when he left Ireland in the year of the Lord 563 and his subsequent travels remain hypothetical. Occasionally, history and hagiography coincide and reinforce each other in confirming his movements. We may wonder at his subduing the Loch Ness monster, but we can accept that he visited Brude, the High King of the Picts at Inverness. But why he chose Iona as his centre of operations remains something of a mystery. We cannot even be sure whether it was ceded to him by some indifferent Pictish overlord or granted him by a kinsman, King Connal of Dalriada. This territory which corresponds roughly to Argyllshire had already been settled by yet another Irishman, Fergus MacErc, who arrived from Antrim about a hundred years before Columba. In theory, the people of Dalriada were by then Christians, as were some of the Picts. But this conversion had been carried out piecemeal, from small isolated cashels and solitary hermitages. In time, the faith had faded as the holy men died off and were not replaced. To revive it was only part of Columba's mission: his plan was to unify the country as well as spread the gospel. In his attempt to carry it out, he must have travelled extensively, under sail where the winds were favourable, rowed by his solid young monks when they were not. Many of his reported miracles deal with defeating storms at sea. So he would have been familiar with the many moods of the local waters, especially with the Firth of Lorn, that long corridor of Scottish history which takes its name from one of King Fergus' brothers (Loarn).

Tourists from Oban travelling down the Firth the forty miles to Colonsay will recognise some of its features – the stretch along Kerrera, for instance, and if they have already made the crossing to Craignure, bound perhaps for Iona, the long reach of the Ross of Mull which borders the Firth to the south. To the east lies the island of Seil, with the Clachan bridge, built towards the end of the eighteenth century, which links it to the mainland and gives rise to the popular joke about 'crossing the Atlantic on foot'. To some, Seil is more memorable for the inn which served the ferry in the old days: it is called Tigh an Truish, the House of Trousers. The ban on the wearing of the kilt, imposed after the Risings, was soon lifted in favour of the Highland regiments because it was believed that this symbol of their national identity would strengthen their fighting spirit. So on the battlefields the world over,

112

from Europe to America to India, Fraser's Highlanders, and Keith's, Campbell's regiment and MacDonald's, MacLeods, Camerons, Gordons, Seaforth or Sunderland swung into action in the dress of their forbears. But when they came home on leave, the ban was re-imposed. Men returning from the wars had to change into the civilian garb, trousers or breeches, imposed by law, leaving their tartan 'uniform' carefully stored in the presses provided by inns who saw some profit to be made from the sartorial regulations.

After Seil and its little outlier, Easdale, once famous for its slate quarries, come Luing, hiding Shuna and its woods to the east and to the west Lunga, circled by tiny islets, then Scarba, a massive and barren mountain top rising about fifteen hundred feet from its base on the sea bed fathoms below, its rugged outline unmistakable among the dozens of islands recognised only by seasoned travellers. Scarba is not as rebarbative as it may first appear. Sailing under it, Bowman found it 'a very picturesque object', noting its 'broken crags which are clothed with beautiful heather ... and in the bright sunshine,' he says he could 'distinguish every flower which enamelled its rugged rocks and covered them with beauty'. Scarba has its birds too, cormorants and the rather less common shags, and may have derived its name from the Norse word for the former. It is now virtually uninhabited though it maintained a small population in the last century. The presence of Kilmory lodge over on the more sheltered east coast suggests

a monastic settlement in ancient times. What
buildings there may have been have disappeared without trace but there are many head-
stones in what must have been the graveyard
attached to the vanished chapel on the site
which had a miraculous reputation.

Scarba is separated from Jura, the long
narrow island whose heights close the horizon to the east for the rest of the journey, by
the notorious Gulf of Corryvreckan, the
Cauldron of the Evil One, with its wicked
whirlpool. Next come the Garvellachs, the
Isles of the Sea, the lands of the Firth most
closely associated with St Columba. Strung
out on a line running north-east to south-

west, the four main islands first appear as one; then as the boat sails by, sort themselves out into separate identities – little Dun Chonnuil (Dunconnel) to the north with its old fort and, southernmost, Eileach an Naoimh, known as the Island of the Saint. Is it really the famed Hinba, where an angel appeared to Columba to advise him on settling the succession when King Connal died in 574? The rules of tanistry which then prevailed did not allow for primogeniture – the king's eldest son was not necessarily the heir apparent. Younger sons, step-sons, bastards occasionally and other kinsmen were in the running: in this case the choice was between two brothers, Eogan and Aidan, cousins of the late king. Cuimine the Fair is the first to tell how the matter was determined by heavenly intervention; Adamnan picked the story up later, using very much the same words. 'At another time the holy man, while staying in the island of Hynba, one night, when in an ecstasy of mind, saw an angel of the Lord sent unto him, who held in his hand the glass book of the ordination of kings. This book he received from the hand of the angel, and began to read. Refusing to ordain Aidan king as he was directed (for he loved his brother more), the angel suddenly stretched forth his hand and smote the Saint with a whip, the mark of the bruise whereof remained on his side all the days of his life.' The angel threatened to renew the whipping and, as Cuimine says, 'The Saint sailed over to the Island of Iona, and Aidan coming thither, he ordained him king.' That Aidan succeeded Connal we can at least accept as fact. Whether or not this most memorable of Columba's several encounters with angels did take place in the Garvellachs, there is plenty of evidence to associate the saint and his mission with Eileach an Naoimh. Folk memory ascribes a sacred spring to him; practically the only feasible landing-place on the island, a narrow inlet on the south-east coast protected by the so-called Dark Skerries has been named after him, Port Columcille. Near the port are important remains of a monastic foundation. The ruins of a chapel, a tiny cell even, domestic buildings to serve as the monks' liv-

116

ing quarters, an enclosure which may have been their herb garden, a possible burial ground and the vallum, or boundary wall which marked out the limits of the establishment, date back no further than the ninth century. However, they include a grave in the Irish style with its low entrance and underground chamber marked by a cross of the type carved in the seventh century. This is the reputed burial place of Columba's mother, Eithne. The site on which these relics stand is held to have been first chosen and developed by Columba's friend and slightly older contemporary, St Brendan of Clonfert. When Brendan sought solitude, it is said that he retired to his hermit's cell on another of the Garvellachs, the small island of A'Chuli which lies south of Dunconnel; further up the Firth he is remembered by the shores of Loch Seil where he liked to rest from his travels on a hillock known as St Brendan's Seat, while Columba has yet another well on Lunga. Like Scarba, Lunga is a Norse word meaning the 'Island of the Longships' and recalling, not the Celtic church but the Viking raids (and possible settlements) which might well have destroyed it. Up and down the Firth of Lorn the religious and the secular meet and mingle and clash – in the Garvellachs, the Isle of the Saint remains a centre of the Columban cult; Dunconnel is remembered for its castle where in the fourteenth century the Macleans having kidnapped John, Lord of the Isles, and King of the Hebrides, held him prisoner till he acceded to their demands. This startling behaviour earned them their lands in Mull, with the strongplaces of Duart and Loch Buie, and, for good measure, the hand of his daughter in marriage. In spite of subsequent vicissitudes, a Maclean still holds the hereditary title of Keeper of the Castle (of Dunconnel). Past the Garvellachs and out in the open sea, there are only a few miles left to Colonsay where the ferry soon drops anchor at Scalasaig.

About Scalasaig itself, opinions differ. Missing the flurry of bigger landing-stages, some find it too remote and, without any striking landmark, insignificant. For me, it sums up the spaciousness of the Inner Hebrides, where there is always room – and time – to idle the hours away watching the scenery change with the light. There seems to be a special quality of tranquillity about Scalasaig which is no more than a cluster of small houses, neatly whitewashed. Thirty years ago its population was reckoned to be forty-five; nowadays the whole island has hardly more than twice the number. Scalasaig has a shop and a post office which sells groceries and cigarettes and postcards and apples and sweets and, three times a week when the ferry from Oban comes in, newspapers. From the pier, the road climbs the hillside to the pretty church with its belfry built in 1802. Facing it and overlooking the harbour is Colonsay's only hotel, another listed building with a vivid garden. The ferry hurrying off again on its return journey to the mainland leaves behind some small craft moored alongside the pier; across the waters of the bay, a headland ends in a 'Stevenson' lighthouse shaped like a drum. Beset by seagulls it looks out to the mountains of Jura. The coast is rocky, full of glittering pools busy with sea-birds and just enough grass for the odd sheep to graze among them. As often as not a rainbow stretches over the sky to Jura. Passing through Scalasaig, the road runs north and south and, in an eccentric series of loops, covers the west coast as well. It is complemented by reasonably well-defined tracks which lead across the moor to Colonsay's many antiquities – all sorts of standing stones, the ruins of duns, cairns, what is left of ancient churches and chapels and other holy sites, burial grounds, including an unusual Viking one. By these tracks one can reach deserted beaches, Balnahard Bay, for instance, up in the north-east corner, one of the most isolated parts of Colonsay which can

Wild Goats

119

be approached only on foot or by boat. There are wild goats on the dunes and cowrie shells on the sands. Tracks too make it possible to climb Colonsay's few hills, including Ben nan Gudairean, which is not far short of 500 feet. Below it and slightly to the north lies Colonsay's main stretch of inland water, Loch Fadda, long and narrow and running in two sections from the grounds of Colonsay House to Kilchattan. The views from the top of Gudairean are very fine and on a clear day, it is just possible to detect the Irish coast.

Which brings us back to St Columba and his connection with Colonsay, often taken to have been named after him, as Oronsay is said to have been called after St Oran. Some even spell the latter Oransay, not Oronsay, to make their point. There are, however, a number of tidal islands in the Hebrides of the same name (though spellings vary) which refers to a peninsula. It is in fact on Oronsay, not Colonsay, that Columba is reported to have landed. There, they say, he climbed its one hill, saw Ireland over on the western horizon and, faithful to his vow of never settling within sight of his native land, travelled on. Ben Oronsay, however, is hardly more than 300 feet, and could hardly have afforded so extensive a view: Ben Gudairean seems a more appropriate venue for this famous incident, the first of several. Besides, as modern sceptics point out, Colonsay's east coast is easier of access by sea than Oronsay's which is hemmed in by skerries. Yet the two together would surely have provided him with a better base than Iona, if only because much bigger. Though fairly fertile, Iona is so small that it can hardly have had resources enough for its own tiny population, let alone have been expected to feed an influx of hungry monks. The mystery of Iona remains and later generations have been thrown back on to legend to solve it. But choose it he did, and having once made certain that Ireland was at last out of sight, had his vessel buried in the sands to remove any lingering temptation to break his vow. There must have been more to it than that: the distance from Dunadd, King Connal's capital, the proximity of the Picts would have been considered and other political factors have played their part. Yet it is not beyond belief that in a superstitious age when oaths were neither taken nor broken lightly Columba should have felt himself bound by his word. Indeed, there is a tradition that when he did return to Ireland in 575 (accompanying the new King Aidan of Dalriada to the important convention of Drum Ceatt) he travelled blindfold so that it might not be said that he ever 'saw' Ireland again. Most of the contemporary evidence there may once have been – from sacred buildings to sacred texts – has either vanished or been destroyed; only tradition is left. But the Celtic Church Columba established lived on for several centuries and his aura was such that nearly every island claims a visitation, if not by the saint himself, at least by one of the founding fathers. On Colonsay, for instance, Kiloran Bay suggests a more convincing association with St Oran than does Oronsay itself. Leaving religious history aside, it is one of the most spectacular sites on Colonsay. A mile of virgin sands ruffled only by the tide spreads out in a silver crescent between lofty headlands. Except at the height of the holiday season, the beach is generally deserted; after that, I am told, the locals claim it as their own and rather resent any intrusion by 'foreigners'. On a fine day, one walks down the gentle slope from the moor to paddle at the water's edge, turning back on one's own track to admire a Man Friday's set of solitary footprints; when the weather changes, there is the awe-inspiring sight of the great Atlantic rollers thundering in. To get another view of Kiloran, the best perhaps, means climbing the steep path which leads up to the crofthouses scattered round Uragaig. Over the sea is the Ross of Mull, backed by the mountains of the Ben More range, with Iona just round the corner. This is a land of high cliffs, a two-mile ridge of rock rising vertically and fractured by caves, and of the so-called raised beaches, strands isolated as the level of the sea dropped in a complicated geological process which marked the end of the Ice Age. At Uragaig the beaches are more than a hundred feet above the coast line which is estimated to have found its present level about 5,000 BC. Other examples of these sandy platforms are to be found on the south-east coast (between Baleromindubh and Balerominmore) and on Oronsay. To the south of Uraigaig lies Loch an Sgoltaire, the largest stretch of inland water after the Fadda lochs. It is well stocked with brown trout and with quite a lot of history attached to the ruins of a small fort on one of its islets. East of Kiloran bay the heights of Carnan Eain match Ben Gudairean; on its slopes are the well-defined ruins of a small cairn.

The track which leads on to Balnahard passes a Viking burial site which is unusual in that it contains not only the longship that covered the human corpse but the skeleton of a horse. When it was excavated in 1881, parts of its harness were found as well. The implements buried with their owner include a set of scales which suggest that he was a merchant travelling the Hebrides in the ninth or tenth centuries, and that in turn indicates that the raiding Norsemen were being replaced by settlers. About a dozen sites in all have been excavated in Colonsay and Oronsay, uncovering similar evidence of peaceful activity. In the machair of the central Machrins region and elsewhere, domestic implements have been found – knives, pins and needles made of bone, a quern for grinding grain, even an iron nail – as well as a variety of beautiful brooches. But most of the artefacts have been removed to museums and the sand has blown over the graves that held them.

Those in search of holy sites and religious remains will find St Columba's well in a gulley near the north-east end of Kiloran Bay and another 3 miles along, all that is left of a chapel with its burial ground dedicated to St Catriona, otherwise known as St Catherine of

Alexandria. The enclosure is well marked by
a ring of boulders. There is a tradition that a
convent once stood here and that the standing-stone north of the boundary was used as a
whipping post for peccant nuns. The stone,
and another one nearby, have been dated back
to the Bronze Age. Though legend often dis-
torts history, there is generally enough left of
the ruins of Colonsay and Oronsay for their
past to be reconstructed, at least by archaeologists. But of St Oran's settlement there is
hardly a trace. What evidence there may have
been of a monastic establishment has been
destroyed – not in the Viking raids or other
accidents of warfare, but by the mindless

vandalism of later generations. Kiloran Abbey is believed to have stood near the present Colonsay House – a good, plain Georgian mansion built in 1722 from the very stones of the abbey. All that is now left to recall St Oran is the well named after him in the grounds.

Colonsay House is famous for its gardens which (unlike the house) are open to the public. The rhododendrons are justly famous and such semi-tropicals as mimosa, palms and eucalyptus testify to the mildness of the climate. A right of way off the last stretch of the road to Kiloran leads to them: it crosses fields and meadows into the woods where bluebells carpet the glades, ferns uncurl, wild irises grow thick by the water. In season, the rhododendrons and exotic blooms make a rich display; and the trees are always there 'lovely, lonesome, cool and green'. Pennant admired them in 1772; there were further plantations of elm, ash, birch and sycamore in the 1830s. But the wind remains the enemy.

When Colonsay House and its pleasure gardens were being established, the MacNeills were the owners, Malcolm MacNeill, who built the house, having bought the lands early in the eighteenth century from the first Duke of Argyll, for Colonsay, like so many of the other islands, had been held by the Campbells, in this case since the days of James the Sixth. Their tenure had not been uninterrupted: the execution of the 9th earl who had supported the Monmouth rebellion in 1685 had brought it to a temporary end. However, the 10th earl, who became the first duke, sided with William of Orange and regained his estates. For their part, the MacNeills had also been embroiled in the political turmoil of the seventeenth century, but it seemed they were now content with their role as landed proprietors. They had taken no part in the Stuart risings. Yet it seems that Malcolm MacNeill's son Donald once received a visit that was not altogether welcome: according to an old tradition, Prince Charles Edward called at Colonsay House in search of support. The story they tell on Colonsay, involving hidden treasure, contradicts the received facts, but it is an exciting one which may have slipped through the official records. It is generally agreed that sailing from France in the summer of 1745, the Prince first landed in the Outer Hebrides. But the long oral tradition passed on through the generations holds that he interrupted his voyage at Colonsay. He had with him, they say, a large, secret sum of money to aid his enterprise and wished to hide it 'in the heather' till it was needed. Landing at the little island of Olmsa, a couple of miles north of Scalasaig and having sent an emissary to Colonsay House, he then went there himself to plead his cause. All he now asked for were local pilots who could help negotiate the difficult crossing to Barra. Having refused to take responsibility for the Prince's treasure, MacNeill acceded to this. Volunteers presented themselves, two Mac-Millan brothers. They went on board, then one lost heart and slipped away with the little keg of gold pieces which was to have been his reward for guiding the Prince. Eventually, this money is said to have been used to assist his descendants to settle in Canada. The tale, true or false, is told in more detail in Norman Newton's book on Colonsay.

A sentimental journey to Olmsa can be made only by the sea-going – or the very determined; the whole north-east coast is virtually inaccessible from Balnahard with its wild goats – like the Rhum ponies possible descendants of Spanish stock from the Armada – all the way down to Scalasaig, there is neither road nor path through the moor. This means that most visitors will also

miss a late instance of 'clearances' – at Riska-
buie, a now deserted fishing village whose
inhabitants were removed at the end of the
First World War to be re-housed (at Glas-
saird) on the outskirts of Scalasaig. The area,
more properly Riasg Bhuide, the Yellow
Moss, is an ancient one which has yielded up
a notable, and very beautiful, Pictish Cross.
Once it had a chapel, pulled down in part to
provide stones to build the cottages and, older
still, there are standing stones nearby. A historical oddity to the north of Olmsa is also
difficult to reach – this is Dunan nan Nighean,
the fort of the daughters, set aside for the
wives of MacDuffie chieftains when they
were about to give birth and where, it is said,
seven females of the family were born.

Even by the complex standards of Scottish
clans, the MacDuffie lineage is more than
usually difficult to unravel. This is partly
because of the many variants of the name
itself, ranging from MacPhee or MacFie to
Macguffie and Machaffie (the latter with yet
another spelling in Ireland). According to the
records, a Donald MacDuffie was there to
participate in the signing of the Charter of
Dingwall in the fifteenth century and, in the
seventeenth, Malcolm MacFie of Colonsay
lost his life at the hands of the MacDonalds.
In its Gaelic form of Mac-Dubh-shithe, the
name means 'son of the dark man' and this
has been taken to indicate that the clan's
ancestor may have been a monk (in his dark
robes), perhaps an abbot of Iona. But again,
the reference to 'dark' may refer to black

magic or sorcery and folklore has many stories involving the MacDuffies with witchcraft, though sometimes as its victims. There was the handsome young MacDuffie who fell into the clutches of the 'Old Woman of Jura' who kept him prisoner by means of a magic ball of thread which she threw into his boat whenever he tried to escape. A black dog with supernatural powers (a common feature in Scottish legend) makes his appearance; so does a miraculous staff on which the fate of the clan depended. And Martin records a previous stone from a crucifix at Oronsay in the possession of 'Mack-Duffie' which he says was held to cure all diseases – surely an example of white magic. But although the early history of the clan may remain unknown, there is no doubt that MacDuffies (or MacPhees) of Colonsay were its lairds until it passed through the fortunes of war into the hands of the Mac-Donalds, then to the MacNeills who held it until the end of the nineteenth century (when it was acquired by the Lords Strathcona and Mount Royal whose ancestor founded the Canadian Pacific Railway).

The ruined fortress taken to be the MacDuffie's ancestral seat is Dunevin (Dunn Eibhinn), whose considerable remains including the defensive walls, are clearly silhouetted from the road about a mile west of Scalasaig. 'Lord of Dunevin' was the title accorded to Malcolm MacDuffie on a sixteenth century grave-slab at Oronsay Priory. But the stronghold probably dates much further back if we are to believe Martin when he tells us that 'the

Natives have a Tradition among them, of a very little Generation of People, that once lived here, call'd Lusbirdan, the same with Pigmies', which suggests that Colonsay may already have been populated in prehistoric times. Martin also describes another hill-fort, known as Dun Cholla. 'There are likewise several Forts here, one of which is call'd Duncoll; it is near the middle of the Isle, it hath large Stones in it, and the Wall is seven Foot broad.' It is in fact between the track that leads to Balerominmore and the main road to the Strand and Oronsay. These two forts, along with Dombnuill on Oronsay itself, may have formed part of the kind of early warning system which, in the north of the Firth of Lorn, linked the coast of Morvern to the castles of Oban and Mull.

Ancient strongholds are lavishly scattered throughout Colonsay, thirteen in all, and however little is left of them, are worth visiting for their beautiful surroundings. The same applies to its standing stones, those still mysterious pillars, some now standing alone, others in the remnant of circles, which are generally taken to have played a central part in the early cult of sun-worship. In Colonsay, some of the stones are associated with history and legend. Thus 'Fingal's Limpet Hammers', the tall stones at the west end of Loch Fadda near Kilchattan, bring together the great mythological hero with the common practice of eating shell-fish in times of scarcity. Unlike other sea-folk, the islanders of the Hebrides thought little of such fare, not prizing even their native lobsters and oysters and crabs, and eating crustaceans only when all else failed. However, they had devised a small stone instrument to dislodge limpets from the rocks which bears some resemblance to the Hammers. Another locally famous stone, known as MacFie's, which stands by Balerominmore and its old burial ground, recalls a bloody incident in the clan's territorial dispute with the MacDonalds. In 1623, Malcom MacDuffie, the last chieftain, was detected as he tried to make his escape across the Strand, dragged back and stood against the stone to be shot. This 'crewall Slauchter' in which several of his followers were also put to death, brought an end to the clan's hold on Colonsay. The stone itself, several times knocked down, badly damaged and carelessly restored, is engraved with the cross motif, a common practice when the Columban church took over Druidic monuments and 'converted' them, as it were. But how old MacFie's stone is has not been satisfactorily established. On the other side of the Strand, near Garvard, a standing-stone (re-erected in the 1960s) and what appears to be the remains of a circle are associated with the administration of justice in the Middle Ages, of which there is a brutal reminder in the Hangman's Rock east of the tidal flats. At the flats, the reach known as the Strand, the easy ramblings enjoyed on Colonsay come to an end, for the new experience which lies ahead at Oronsay Priory depends on the tide and needs careful planning.

Oronsay Priory

The crossing of the Strand provides an attractive introduction: over a mile long stretch of sands (and sharp shingle which make protective footwear advisable), round and through glittering pools, with a low line of irregular reefs to the south, and to the north the moor from which projects the elongated rock known locally as the Elephant's Trunk. Past it and back on dry land, a steep, unmetalled road climbs the hill, then wanders on through grazing land till, round a bend, the Priory comes into sight enclosed by a stone wall and backed by the farm buildings (now in private hands). It stands at the foot of the western slope of Ben Oronsay, erected on

the traditional plan with its church, chapel and chapter-house, its monastic buildings, including dormitory and refectory, and, for recreation, its walks round a cloistered arcade. 'There are several Houses without the Square, which the Monks liv'd in', says Martin, adding: 'There is a Garden at twenty yards distance on the North side of the Houses.' The Church is now roofless, but the strong walls with their elegant lancet windows are still standing, rising to twenty feet. Opening off the church, there was a small mortuary chapel known as the Mac-Duffie Aisle. Their grave-slabs, and those of others equally famous in their day, were removed to the (re-roofed) Prior's House where they stand in arcaded niches along the walls, constituting the Priory's greatest treasure. And with its other treasure, the remarkable Prior Colin's cross, it stands comparison with Iona Abbey as one of Scotland's finest ecclesiastical ruins. Its history, however, is less well documented than the Abbey's.

It was founded in the fourteenth century – at some time between 1325 and 1365 are the dates given – by John of Islay, sixth King of the Isles, as a cell of the Abbey of Holyrood, which makes it contemporary with Kidalton on Islay. This act of piety is said to have been made by John in exchange for the Church sanctioning a divorce from his first wife, Amy MacRuari, which enabled him to marry King Robert the Second's daughter, Margaret. Martin, and later travellers, took it for granted that the new Priory replaced a sixth century monastery established either by St Oran or by St Columba. Martin describes it as having been 'built by the famous St Columbus, to which this Church is dedicated'; on his visit in 1772, Pennant referred to it as the monastery of St Oran. Documents of the fourteenth century say the Priory was subject to Kiloran Abbey on Colonsay. But no trace remains of either the Abbey or of any dependency it may have had on Colonsay: we have little but highly unreliable hearsay evidence as to what preceded the Priory. Time has mouldered its fabric and brought roofs down – in Pennant's time it was already open to the skies – but it seems to have escaped the worst

of human depredations even during the
Reformation. Isolated on its few acres of land,
cut off by the high tide, it continued to be
occupied by regular canons – Augustinians,
Cistercians, Benedictines – as prior succeeded
prior, including the MacMhuirichs, Mac-
Phails and, of course, MacDuffies, who in turn
were laid to rest under its famous grave-
stones. But Oronsay Cross still stands tall, 16
feet on its pedestal, seemingly unchanged since
Martin first wrote it up: '... there is a large
Cross on the West side of the Church, of an
entire Stone very hard; there is a Pedestal of
three Steps, by which they ascend to it, it is
sixteen Foot high and Foot and a half broad,
there is a large Crucifix on the West-side of this

Prior Colin's Cross

Cross, it has an Inscription underneath, but not legible, being almost wore off by the Injury of Time; the other side has a Tree engraven on it'. The inscription has been deciphered; translated from the Latin it reads: 'This is the cross of Colinus, son of Christinus Mac-Duffie.' The sculptor identified himself in an inscription on the pedestal: 'Mael-Sechlainn O Cuinn, mason, made this work' – probably in the last quarter of the fifteenth century. The decoration is exceptionally fresh, the Crucifix whole and largely unspoilt, and, adopted from an earlier age, it is embellished by a side-show of fabulous animals whose tails are linked to luxuriant foliage enclosed in a series of roundels. At the other end of the Priory, by the entrance, there is another smaller cross which celebrates a miracle performed by St John the Evangelist. On the upper portion (which belongs to the sixteenth century), the saint is dealing with a transmogrified dragon which has poisoned a chalice. He stands with one hand raised in blessing, the other holding the sacred vessel from which a small beast emerges.

The astonishing actuality of medieval stone carving is seen at its best in the Priory's grave stones. There are about thirty of them, celebrating for posterity the great and powerful of the day. Time has mutilated some of the stones; others have survived in all their vivid detail, among them the grave-slab of Murdoch MacPhee on which a great sword rests point down on a galley in full sail, under a picture of the chase – a group of deer surround a powerfully antlered stag with a hound in close pursuit. There are 'gisants', including a recumbent knight in full armour, and Canon Bricius MacMhuirich is represented with his head on a tasselled pillow supported by angels, his feet resting on a lion. Perhaps the most endearing of all is the effigy of Mariota, 'daughter of Alexander, son of John MacIan'. Evidently a rich and pious laywoman, she wears a caul-like coif, a long robe with wide sleeves over which a cloak is fastened by a circular brooch. She has a book and a rosary, but two small dogs find room to nestle in her lap.

Oronsay has one other fine sight to offer those lucky enough to find a boat – and a knowledgeable pilot – to take them down to Eilean nan Ron at the very end of the skerries which crowd its coast to the east and south and provide a favourite breeding ground for grey Atlantic seals. In season, as many as a thousand converge on these waters and late in the autumn, the rocks are thick with seal-pups placed there under the close supervision of the cows until they are ready to swim. Then the mating starts again, and the roar of the battling bulls can be heard for miles. And where the seal-pup nurseries have left the rocks bare, there is the occasional sight of cormorants or shags – it is difficult for the uninitiated to tell them apart – standing in solemn rows shaking their shoulders to rid their heavy wings of excess water.

Oronsay provides one landing point at Seal Cottage half-way up the coast and from there, it is a pleasant walk over rolling moor to the Priory. From most of Colonsay it is Jura one sees; here Islay dominates the horizon. During the tourist season, some of the ferries from Oban to Colonsay call at Port Askaig on their way; earlier and later in the year, it is back to the mainland for those planning to continue exploring the Southern Hebrides. Geographically Colonsay and Islay are linked, along with Jura and little Gigha,

Shag and chick

and once upon a time it seems that the connection was closer – at least according to
legend. A holy well on Colonsay took
umbrage when a local woman used it to wash
her hands. So it dried up and took itself off to
Islay where it is known as Tobar na Cnabar,
which roughly translated means 'the well that
moved away'.

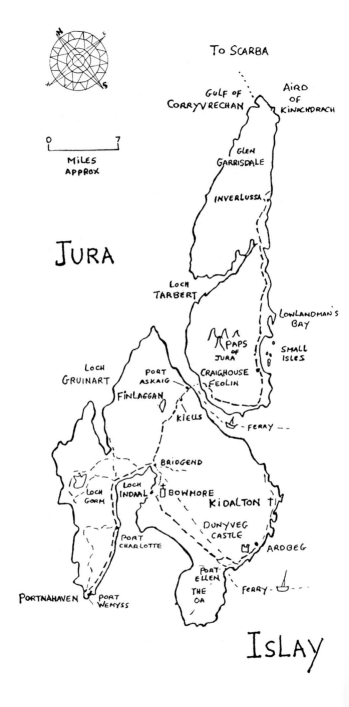

VII

Roads to The Isles (3) – Kintyre and Beyond – Jura, Islay, Gigha

Tarbert's Harbour Street fronts the working area of its deep horseshoe bay which is practically closed off from its exit into the wide and turbulent waters of Loch Fyne. It is the town's main street, with restaurants and hotels and pubs side by side with the butcher, the baker and the ship's chandler. The pier where the fishing boats congregate is just across the road, cluttered with nets and pots and all the usual tackle of a busy port. From the eighteenth century onwards Tarbert was the headquarters of Loch Fyne's fishing industry; it still maintains its fleet as well as harbouring deep sea trawlers from the east coast. An unusual feature is the square-ish artificial island, known locally as the 'Beilding'. It was put up to help sailing vessels negotiate the narrow entrance to the bay, winching them in against contrary winds. On the far side a flotilla of prettily painted pleasure boats waits upon the weather, others finding independent moorings are dispersed over the water. Tarbert is a well-known rendezvous for yachtsmen, with its yacht club at the far end of the town where in rough weather white 'sea-horses' from Loch Fyne come racing in. Here attempts were made to build a pier but abandoned when a gale swept it away.

Tarbert

The waters of Tarbert are known as the
East Loch; over the hill, past the Victorian
Gothic church with its massive crowned
tower, lies the West Loch, long and quiet and
narrow. The main road down the west coast
of Kintyre runs along it to the open sea, with
Islay and Gigha over the water, which is
closed to the north by the mountains of Jura.
The narrow isthmus between the two lochs
has played its part in history: in 1098, Magnus
Barelegs had his galleys dragged across it in
order to fulfil to the letter the treaty he had
extracted from gentle King Edgar, known as
the Peaceable, by which he would be entitled
to add to his Hebridean kingdom any lands

142

that he could circumnavigate. History books
– or some of them – tell us that more than two
hundred years later Robert the Bruce emu-
lated this feat, travelling in reverse direction,
coming to Tarbert where he erected its other
landmark, the castle sometimes called after
him. Its ruins now stand sharply defined high
on the moor over the town. The Bruce no
doubt occupied it and may well have
extended it, but its foundations pre-date him.
It is after all unlikely that a site of such
obvious strategic importance should have
been ignored, and there are records of a hill-
fort on the emplacement as early as the eighth
century. What is now left of the castle owes

more to James the Fourth who stayed there during his many attempts to gain control of the Western Highlands and their seaboard.

Through the centuries, Tarbert has had its ups and downs – an important military and administrative centre as long as the Lordship of the Isles lasted, by the fourteenth century it had gained the status of a royal burgh. Then history seems to have passed it by, its castle losing its importance when peaceful times came to the West Coast. In the seventeenth century, with the rest of Kintyre it came under the control of the Earl of Argyll who brought in Lowlanders from Ayrshire. It flourished again in the eighteenth century along with the Campbell capital, Inveraray, and the herring trade. But fish are fickle and the great shoals are no more. Now Tarbert profits from its position high up on Kintyre and near the ferry for Islay. A steady stream of tourists make Tarbert a staging-post, but they say that you must have at least four generations of local fishermen among your ancestors before being considered anything but a 'foreigner'

For southerners setting out on a tour of the Inner Hebrides from Islay, Glasgow is the obvious starting-point. No trains run up the south-west coast, but on a fine day the half-hour flight to Campbeltown down by the Mull of Kintyre offers a splendid panorama of islands; the journey by road is even more varied. As the crow flies it is hardly more than forty miles; by road, it is nearer a hundred. By car or by the comfortable coaches which provide most of the public transport, the first part of the journey once past Dumbarton is up Loch Lomond to Tarbet, on the bankside beneath Ben Lomond and the Cobbler, then across to Arrochar to round the head of Loch Long and on to Inveraray with its castle and woods, the beautiful bridge over the river Aray and Georgian town on the shores of Loch Fyne. On the way to the next main stop at Lochgilphead, the road runs by the old village of Furnace with its ironstone quarries which became a centre of iron smelting in the eighteenth century – as its name suggests. The blast furnace still standing serves as yet another reminder that industry came early even to the Highlands to the detriment of its woodlands.

Lochgilphead introduces the district of Knapdale as Tarbert does Kintyre. Once just another small fishing village, it now has six thousand inhabitants and serves as administrative capital for the vast territory of Argyll and Bute. It is essentially a Victorian town, growing in size and importance throughout the nineteenth century when the opening of the Crinan Canal brought both trade and tourists. There are no notable buildings and few tangible reminders of the past, but the town is pleasantly laid out; its wide main street busy with small shops runs down to the shore. The 'front' is tree-lined, a well-tended green slopes down to the water's edge. Behind the screen of trees, the 'buses drive along the road north through Knapdale with its forest and fine coastal scenery the forty miles or so to Oban or take the southern route into Kintyre. The Canal is only a few minutes walk away with its inviting towpath by the loch-keeper's house across the Miller's bridge. From there it runs for eight miles to Crinan where it opens out into the Sea of the Hebrides, while the path leads back for a mile to its head at Ardishraig. For those who believe that nothing is more worthwhile than messing about in boats – or better still, watching others do so – a stroll along the Canal is a must; a visit to Dunadd, on the other hand, is more of a pious pilgrimage back into history. Off the main road north a farmland track crosses the bog once known as the Crinan Moss and a rocky outcrop rises over the little river Add which winds away to join the Canal. It is a stiff scramble to the top (more than 150 feet) where, stone merging into rock, there is not much left of the great stronghold at the centre of one of Scotland's oldest capitals. Given its position, looking out to sea over several miles of open country which no foe could cross unseen, Dunadd must have been occupied long before Fergus MacErc arrived with his Scots, as the Romans called the Northern Irish, to carve out the kingdom of Dalriada and eventually to give the name of his people to the whole country. The kingdom Fergus founded lasted about three hundred years, from the sixth to the ninth century, but all that is now left at Dunadd are two symbols – the image of a boar delicately carved in relief (and covered with glass for protection) and, embedded in the rock, the mark of a footprint which is associated with coronation ceremonies during which oaths of loyalty were taken to and by the newly appointed king. The ruins of Dunadd reveal no more than glimpses of the past, just enough to leave one wondering, but there are magnificient views to the coast and beyond over a tangle of islands and islets with the mountains of Jura as a background, and further north, the outline of the great Cruachan range.

Back on the coast road south through Tarbert, the choice now lies between visiting Jura or spending time on Islay first. The rest of Kintyre must wait for another occasion for there are practically no roads across the peninsula to the east coast which faces the isle of Arran. For the islands lying to the west, the ferries run from Kennacraig, a landing-stage with neither shop nor hotel. There are two or three sailings a day to Islay, to Port Ellen in the south and Port Askaig up in the north-east where another ferry (Western) plies back and forth across the narrows to Jura. Which of Islay's ports one decides to sail to doesn't really matter for there are good roads – and 'buses – between them, but those who choose Port Askaig are rewarded with the immediate sight of one of the most famous landmarks in the Southern Hebrides – the Paps of Jura. The twin mountains, snow-streaked till late in the spring, rise side by side in perfect symmetry; on a fine day they seem near enough to touch by reaching out a hand. The effect is doubly illusory for the Paps are part of a range of

Jura from Colonsay

seven peaks of which the three highest are
well over two thousand feet. Some guide
books in fact refer to the three Paps and from
certain angles, they are clear to see – from
Bowmore, for instance, across Loch Indaal.
Three is accurate but rather spoils the picture
of the great breasts of a giantess reclining.
Apart from their beauty, the Paps serve well
to suggest the nature of Jura, a large island
about 27 miles long by 6 or 7 across, made up
mainly of mountain and rock, with a wild,
unapproachable west coast of cliffs and coves,
skerries, raised beaches and waterfalls. Martin
describes Jura and the Paps as follows: 'The
Isle is mountainous along the middle, where

there are four Hills of considerable height; the
two highest are well-known to Sea-faring
Men, by the name of the Paps of Jura; they are
very conspicuous from all Quarters of Sea
and Land in these Parts.' The entry is an
unusually long one, full of what the century
would have called curiosities, such as the lon-
gevity of the inhabitants. 'Several of the
Natives have liv'd to a great Age: I was told
that one of them, called Gillovir Mack-Crain,
liv'd to have kept one hundred and eight
Christmases in his own Home.' He died in
the reign of Charles the First and was buried
at Kilearnadil; he is also mentioned on the
headstone over the grave of one of his descen-

dants, Mary MacCrain, who died in 1865 at the age of 128 and lies in the cemetery at Inverlussa (Kilchianain). Martin also quotes the case of an incomer: 'Bailiff Campbell lived to the Age of one hundred and six years, he died three Years ago, he passed the thirty three last Years before his Death in this Isle.' The Bailiff no doubt benefited from the climate which Martin esteemed salubrious above all: 'This Isle is perhaps the wholesomest Plat of Ground either in the Isles or Continent of Scotland, as appears by the long Life of the Natives, and their State of Health; to which the Height of the Hills is believ'd to contribute in large measure, by the fresh Breezes of wind that come from 'em to purify the Air.'

Pennant, another traveller who took seriously the job of recording what he saw, was more struck, however, by the wretched condition in which the people of Jura lived and by their miserable fare that seemed to include a regular diet of the despised limpets and winkles which he watched the women and children gather along the shore. The poverty of their habitations, 'black houses' still without a chimney, the meagreness of their crops – barley, oats, potatoes – shocked him and he attributed them to the poverty of the soil in this 'most rugged of the Hebrides'. Pennant also found the time, and the energy, to climb the highest of the Paps. It was heavy going, but he was rewarded by the views. From the summit of Ben-an-Oir, at 2,571 feet, he described Jura spread out below as 'a stupendous scene of rock, varied with little lakes innumerable'. The horizon to the north-east was rimmed by Ben Lomond, to the south, by the Firth of Clyde and the distant coast of North Ireland, with all the islands scattered over the sea – Islay, Gigha and Arran, Colonsay with Oronsay, Mull, Iona and the 'long extent of Tirey and Col'. Pennant also identified the 'Slide of the Old Hag' on the western side of the mountain, a long and narrow strip of rock falling away precipitously into the sea. Here the witch fell to her death as she pursued her young MacPhee lover who having broken the spell at last made his escape over the Sound.

The explorer, Sir Joseph Banks, who had preceded Pennant, climbed only the lesser southern range; Bowman viewed Jura from the sea, but did not land. His diary entry confirms the general impression of barrenness: 'Before us was the long island of Jura with its three absolutely conical mountains, significantly called the Paps of Jura, rising from the southern part of it to the height of about 2,500 feet. This island seemed little more than one continuous mountainous ridge.' What Bowman most enjoyed, it seems, was his breakfast; 'We breakfasted in the northern part of the Sound of Jura, on fresh herrings as white as snow. They who have not eaten herrings immediately after being taken, cannot conceive their excellence.'

Neglect of Jura, or indifference, is nothing new: in the seventeenth century, Sir James Turner had already been put off by its apparent infertility – a 'horrid ile', he called it, fit only for deer. The deer are still there, on the privately owned 'sporting estates' which occupy most of Jura. Statistics are hard to come by and difficult to interpret partly because it has been the custom to lump together some of the less populated islands, Scarba and the Garvellachs with Jura, for instance. But the figures we have tell their own story – in 1851, Jura supported 948 people, much the same as it had done a hundred years before; in 1971, the population was down to 200, a fifth of the number who had lived there two centuries earlier. It is true that Pennant deplored the natives' circumstances, but the fact remains that 'black cattle' was raised in now deserted glens and one thousand head a year were exported to the mainland. They left for Knapdale from Lagg, then a sizeable township with its annual fair. It owed its pier to Thomas Telford, who was also responsible for the piers at Craighouse and Feolin. Throughout the nineteenth century Jura was much better provided with harbours than it is now when only Feolin survives (its facilities subsidised by the European Community). As Jura became more cut off its amenities decreased – schools and inns, the old 'change houses', were closed, churches emptied, their overgrown churchyards falling into disuse, its many craftsmen and small traders shut up shop. As elsewhere in the islands, the sheep that were brought in displaced the people and eventually overcropped and ruined the land. Ships bound for the Americas came to carry off whole families, the first leaving as early as 1739. There was another wave of emigration in the 1830s and 1840s when the potato crop failed. The wreck of one of these ships can still be seen on the Corran Sands – according to tradition she was the *Agnes* come to collect emigrants from Jura in the 1860s. How many of them left voluntarily in search of a better life and how many were literally evicted to make way for sheep, and later for deer, remains in dispute. But there is a long list of place names as evidence of displacement and depopulation. Not only Lagg, but Kinnuach-drach harbour in the north-east is empty; further down the coast, Lussagiven has shared the fate of other ports once active. The fishing community settled at Cruib on the northern shore of Loch Tarbert to exploit the herring catch left long ago, no-one now lives at Ruan-tallan near the mouth of the loch. In the south by Jura House, a former settlement at Bros-dale has all but vanished, leaving the deserted farmhouse as Sunnaig as witness. Many other villages have been written off – among them Cnocbreak, Carn and Leargybreak. The local historian John Mercer and others have no doubt that their people were 'cleared' in order to turn the surrounding woods into a deer forest. For Jura has had the double misfortune of being taken over first for sheep farming, then for game. As its most famous visitor, George Orwell, said, the two enemies of the people of Jura are landlords and deer.

Jura's connection with deer is an old one for

'The enemy of the people'

it is generally accepted that it got its name
from the Norse word for the red deer that the
Vikings hunted there. There are other,
perhaps more fanciful, interpretations: some
say the name Jura comes from the Gaelic
word for 'yew tree' though it is not on record
that yews ever grew there in unusual
numbers; others, that Jura rather than the
Garvellachs was the fabled Hinba. Martin was
told the legend, already old in his day,
according to which two Danish brothers, Dih
and Rah fell out and fought to the death near
Knockrome where they were buried under
adjacent standing stones, the phonetic transli-
teration of their name sounding something
like Jura. The most interesting thing about
this story is its ancient association with the
Norsemen whose influence pervades Jura and

prevails over the Columban aura. History records a great battle fought on Jura in the seventh century between the resident Picts and the Scottish invaders who founded Dalriada and the chances are that under rule from Dunadd, Jura was converted to Christianity. But with a single exception there is nothing to recall even in legend the presence of the monks of Iona – no ruins, no relics, no miracles. Martin mentions wells with healing powers but none is named after a saint. Until the Reformation, Jura seems to have had only one church, 'ane chapel' as Dean Munro wrote in 1549. It is at Kilearnadil and may have been built by St Earnan, Columba's uncle who is buried there in the ancient graveyard. This is the Earnan who ruled over the settlement founded on the mysterious Hinba, which Adamnan placed in a 'big sea-bay'. There is nothing of the sort on Eileach an Naoimh with which Hinba is usually identified, but both Loch Tarbert and Lowlandman's Bay in particular fit the description. It is said that Earnan asked to be buried on Jura, or Hinba perhaps. He was on Islay when he died but his body was brought over and landed by the rocks in the south known as Leac Earnan. The caves on the west coast offer a convincing, if tenuous, link with Iona, for in stormy weather they served to store the coffins of the great on their way for burial at Oronsay Priory or Iona. The caves are at Ruantallan and significantly Corpach, 'the place of the dead'. They are within reach only of those who can trace the old drove roads and pony tracks, and tackle them; most of the north coast is similarly isolated.

With the Hebridean empire founded by Somerled administered from Islay, his direct descendants, the MacDonalds, held much of Jura. But the north was Maclean territory, centred round Glen Garrisdale where they had their seat at Castle Aros. Nothing of it now remains, even its exact location is doubtful. On the east coast, the Macleans held the lands of Ardlussa which came to them in the fourteenth century through marriage to a daughter of the first Lord of the Isles. In the south, one of the MacDonalds' most important strongholds was on Am Fraoch Eilean, an islet in the Sound of Islay. Some of Claig Castle was still standing in Pennant's day. With its square tower and 9 feet walls it has served to imprison MacDonald foes as well, so they say, as to increase their revenues by extracting a levy on vessels entering the Sound. The MacDonalds and the Macleans, on Jura as elsewhere, fought each other for supremacy between periods of uneasy truce, but there was no truce between the Macleans and the Campbells who replaced the MacDonalds. In 1647, the Macleans were taken by surprise when their look-out failed to reach them in time to warn them that Campbell ships were approaching. Caught by surprise unarmed, they were massacred, only one man escaping by swimming out into the bay and hiding among the rocks, where Maclean's Skull has served as a reminder of the Battle of Glen Garrisdale.

A few miles further up the coast, Breakan's Cave goes back into earlier times and introduces Jura's most famous landmark after the Paps – the Gulf of Corryvreckan and its whirlpool. The tale is told that a Norwegian Prince who was courting the daughter of the King of the Isles was set a task to match any of the Labours of Hercules. To gain her hand he was to spend three days in the Gulf. He took with him three ropes to anchor his boat – the first made of wool broke, so did the second which was made of hemp. But it seemed that the third, woven of the hair of maidens, was holding till suddenly it gave way for one strand was made of the tresses of a girl who only pretended to be a virgin. The young Prince was sucked into the vortex and his body was eventually washed up into the cave called after him. According to some versions of the legend, it was his faithful dog who towed it there. Less romantically, it is said that the name Corryvreckan is derived from the Gaelic word for 'speckled' or 'brindled' which describes the whirlpool's appearance as it starts to become active.

Corryvreckan has been described over and over again, one of the earliest accounts coming from Martin who added some local colour supplied by those who believed that it was controlled by a witch living on Scarba: 'The boiling of the Sea is not above a Pistol-shot distant from the Coast of Scarba Isle, where the white waves meet and spout up; they call it the Kaillach, i.e. an old Hag; and they say that when she puts on her Kerchief, i.e. the whitest waves, it is then reckon'd fatal to approach her.' The whirlpool in action is a fine, a terrifying sight, but it depends on the tides and those who have walked – clambered is a better word – over the last few miles to Carraig More, the island's northern tip, may be faced with no more than the waters of the Sound lapping quietly away. However peaceful they may look they should never be attempted – the maritime authorities have no doubt that they constitute a real and continuing danger. George Orwell ignored the warnings and came close to losing his life and drowning his young companions. While on Jura, already a dying man, he lived at Barnhill, where he wrote 'Nineteen Eighty Four.' It is a lonely farmhouse overlooking the shore a couple of miles south of Kinuachdrach, where the road – or rather the track that continues it from Inverlussa – comes to an end. From there tourists re-enter modern times on Jura's one metalled road which runs down the east coast and south to Feolin ferry. It is a pleasant drive with little traffic and good views out to sea over the low coastline. There is often a fine antlered stag standing still on the moor, a pheasant in full plumage lazing across the road. For those able to stay on Jura, journey's end is reached at Craighouse, hardly the 'capital' but with its fifty or so inhabitants, definitely the biggest centre of population. The village stretches along the shallow bay facing the Small Isles, a circlet of rocky islets just off the coast, and ends in a group of stone cottages called Craigenhouses.

The eighteenth century well (now disused) stands by the bridge; nearby is the old mill which gave Craighouse its former name of Milltown. On the south side, by Telford's pier the hotel fronts the water; now enlarged and modernised, it was known to travellers in the eighteenth century as the Craighouse Inn. There are palm trees on its terrace, and swans drifting by. On the other side of the road is the distillery, one of the first in Scotland to take out a licence, thus legitimising three hundred years and more of mostly illicit trading on record as early as 1502. But quarrels over rent closed the distillery down just before the First World War, and it was not reopened until the 1960s. Isle of Jura single malt is now back on the market where it joins the mainland malts rather than the strongly peat-flavoured ones of Islay. That is only one of the many differences between the two islands.

It takes only a few minutes to sail from Feolin to Port Askaig but the crossing carries one from the old world to the new. Once, when Somerled held court at Finlaggan, Islay and Jura were closely linked, and they still have many features in common. Both are about 26 miles long, but Islay being broader – up to 20 miles at its widest – has by far the larger acreage. It lays no claim to Jura's mountains, most of its hills being less than one thousand feet, but it is by no means flat. Though it has no forest as such, it is pleasantly wooded and well watered by inland lochs and small rivers. Where Loch Tarbert practically bisects Jura, Loch Indaal, running north–south cuts through Islay, giving it a shape difficult to define. As it appears in an early map designed in 1656 for Johannes Blaeu's 'Atlas Novus', it looks something like a thick-set torso on two legs. Again like Jura, Islay has its empty lands – the north coast in particular where no road runs and the long line of hills and moor bare of habitation on the approach through the Sound of Port Askaig.

Not physically dissimilar and sharing much of its history, Islay parts company with Jura by having embraced the twentieth century. Its population of nearly four thousand testifies to its economic success: with nearly twenty times as many people as Jura, Islay is the most densely populated of the Inner Hebrides, coming second only to Lewis in the Outer Islands. Its staple resources are whisky and farming, particularly cattle breeding. On the ferries to Islay nowadays, there are as many businessmen as tourists.

Islay has seven distilleries mostly dating back to the eighteenth or to the first third of the nineteenth centuries, during which the upper classes, deprived of French brandy by the Napoleonic Wars, took to drinking whisky and acquired a taste for it. Laphroaig is probably the best known; Bowmore, founded in 1799, the oldest. All in spectacular settings, Caol Ila is near Port Askaig and Bunnabhain further up the coast with dramatic views out to sea to Colonsay and Mull; Bruichladdich on the west shore of Loch Indaal faces Bowmore; Port Ellen with its own maltings is on the outskirts of the town; on the other side, the coast road leads to Lagavullin and Ardbeg, passing Laphroaig on the way. The latter's name perfectly describes its location: 'the beautiful hollow by the broad bay'. Following the 'whisky trail' visiting Islay's distilleries (most of them open to the public during the summer, and by special arrangement) is as good a way as any of getting to know the island; encountering its malts for the first time will be a new experience for those accustomed to the produce of Speyside and the Tay. Islay whiskies owe their distinct taste to the local peat; they have their devotees who like the smokey flavour and their detractors who find it medicinal. Whether you enjoy them or not, whether you prefer the gentle Bruichladdich to the full-bodied, uncompromising Laphroaig, for would-be connoiseurs there can surely be no better way of spending time than in discussing a dram of malt.

In the old days, most of the local whisky trade was conducted illegally in the area round Ardbeg, a noted haunt of moonlighters and smugglers; now it is big business, another instance of how Islay has adapted itself and as a result relies less on tourism as a main source of revenue. Yet its visitors are the first to benefit from one of the marks of its prosperity – the good network of roads, well-kept and wider than is usual in the Hebrides. For those without their own transport, there is an adequate 'bus service (and a post-bus, of course). But even with a car, stout shoes and

some mildly energetic walking are needed to explore many of the most interesting places. Another sign of Islay's relative, and shared, affluence is shown by the size of its centres of population. In many of the Hebrides it is easy to drive through a township, then stop to find out where it is for the name clearly marked on the map turns out to refer to a scattering of lonely cottages on the moor. On Islay a village is a village with its school and church and general shop, a small town even. Port Askaig, however, is an exception. Hardly a natural harbour, it lies below a high cliff; it consists of a small hotel with a front lawn running down

to the harbour wall, a post office, the harbour master's house, the life-boat station and the pier. A tall Victorian house (Dunlossit) in Scottish Baronial style stands on the cliff among landscaped woods. The road to Port Ellen winds steeply up the hill passing through the substantial villages of Keills and Ballygrant, on its way to Bridgend and Bowmore. At Bridgend it is joined by the other main road along the banks of Loch Indaal through the part of Islay known as the Rhinns to the coastal townships of Port Charlotte, Port Wemyss and Portnahaven.

The past may be made less of on Islay than

elsewhere but it is very much in evidence, in Bridgend for instance whose story probably goes back at least to the days of the Celtic Church. The little town is at the head of Loch Indaal; the road runs over an eighteenth century bridge across the river Sorn; there are some handsome Georgian houses and an old inn. At the centre, Islay House stands in its own extensive grounds. The mansion was built in the seventeenth century by the Campbells of Cawdor and extended during the eighteenth century by another branch of the family, the Campbells of Shawcross. In the nineteenth century it was sold to yet another kinsman, John Morrison, a Glasgow nabob, whose descendants continued to hold it. The factor's house, also Georgian, stands in the grounds along with stables and a pretty dovecot; there are two follies both in the form of crenellated towers, well-tended gardens and woodland. A burn runs through them, which has been engineered to spill out into a waterfall. Once Islay House was known as Killarow, the name given to the parish and its ancient church of which nothing now remains save the burial ground. The medieval church was dedicated to the Celtic missionary, St Maelrubha, who founded a monastery in Applecross in Wester Ross, and some authorities believe that it stood on the site of a similar settlement built in the seventh or eighth centuries. The position would have been attractive, at the centre of a main trade route from Northern Ireland to the Dalriadic territories on the mainland, with Loch Indaal providing a long stretch of sheltered waters and the Sorn valley an easy road to the coast.

Whether or not Maelrubha or one of his followers established himself at Killarow there is no denying the influence of the Celtic church on Islay. On the road to Bridgend, St Columba himself has his 'shrine' – a small ruined chapel surrounded by its graveyard on the moor above the village of Keills, itself a name taken to be a corruption of 'kil', meaning a church.

Past Bridgend, the road continuing along the east bank of Loch Indaal next reaches Bowmore, which soon took over as the capital of Islay after it was built in the eighteenth century by the Campbells of Shawcross. It was in 1767 that Daniel 'the Younger' decided to create a 'new village' at a time when town planning was coming into fashion. He crowned it with his famous round church, which stands in its contemporary graveyard at the top of Main Street looking down over the centre of the town to the pier head on the loch. Two storeys high, it is perfectly circular, with a conical roof and rectangular tower. Some say it was copied from an ancient church in Jerusalem, others that it was inspired by memories of Italy during the Grand Tour; the local story is that it was designed in the round to do away with any corners the Devil might hide in. It cost 'above £700'. Most of Bowmore's old buildings have gone – the distillery with its pagoda roofs is one of the few left standing. But the general plan, a series of rectangles disposed on the

Bowmore Church

hillside and separated by wide streets, has
been preserved and modern buildings kept in
proportion so that the town retains something
of its Georgian air – a rarity in the Hebrides
where the architecture of the eighteenth century and the Regency period is in general
poorly represented. Daniel was a man of his
times, an early 'improver' with a multitude of
interests, artistic, social and economic, and
the tradition ran in the family. They developed Port Ellen in 1821 – it was named after
the wife of one of the Campbell lairds; so was
Port Charlotte. Port Wemyss, with Portnahaven one of a pair of fishing villages on each
side of the river Rainich, was called after a
daughter of the Earl of Wemyss who had
married into the clan. All these preserve the
air of the spaciousness which marks the Age
of Elegance. The two fishing villages are also
worth visiting for their splendid seascapes.

The headland here is protected from the full force of the ocean by a line of reefs and islets haunted by seals and seabirds. From the group known as Frenchman's Rock off the point of Rubha na Faing to yet another Isle Orsay opposite the mouth of the Rainich, the sea breaks ceaselessly in great rollers and huge sweeps of spray. Shipping is warned off by the Rhinns of Islay lighthouse, designed by Robert Stevenson and built in 1825. At the other end of Orsay (sometimes called Oronsay) there are the remains of a chapel traditionally associated with St Oran, with well-preserved walls clearly visible from the coast. There is another ruined chapel at Nereabolls, 3 miles south of Port Charlotte, well worth a visit for the medieval grave slabs in its burial ground. Islay is rich in ecclesiastical remains; it has for instance seventeen crosses, the finest on the other side of the island from the Rhinns, past Port Ellen and Ardbeg.

A path off the main road leads through quiet fields and pasture land to the site of the chapel, now roofless, and its graveyard sheltered by birch and alders where Kidalton Cross stands nine feet high. There is controversy about its age: some authorities argue from the style of its decoration that it belongs to the eighth century or earlier; others hold that it was made in the fourteenth century at the same time that the chapel was built for that John Lord of the Isles who was responsible for Oronsay Priory. Nobody disputes its beauty, and many regard it as the best example of its kind in the whole of Scotland.

Kidalton Cross

It was cut from a single block of the local 'bluestone' and is literally covered with carvings – scrolls and spiral work, bosses, rings and interlacing, serpents, lions, sheep, birds pecking grapes, as well as biblical scenes – David and the lion, Abraham and Isaac, Cain and Abel, the Virgin and Child with angels at their side.

From Kidalton, the track runs on to Claggan Bay, noted for its beautiful pebbles, passing yet another of Islay's many standing stones on its way north to Ardtalla where it peters out. One of the most impressive of these stone tokens of an older religion is to be found on the way back to Port Ellen, on the moor a mile short of the town. It stands fourteen feet high on rough ground against the hills of Cnoc Mor, a 'magic mountain' which was a sacred place in the days of the Druids. Islay has a stone circle too, the Cultoon Circle north of Portnahaven. Three of its fifteen stones are upright – it seems that the remaining twelve which lie nearby were never put into the sockets dug for them, and no-one knows why. A standing stone, a spade-shaped one, keeps watch over Islay's ancient seat of power, the capital of the kings of the Isles from where they ruled their lands. What Dunadd was to Dalriada, Finlaggan became to the Hebrides. What remains has not changed so very much since Martin observed it: 'Loch-Finlaggan about three miles in circumference ... lies in the Centre of the Isle. The Isle Finlaggan, from which the Lake hath its Name, is in it. It's famous for being once the Court in which the great Mack-Donald, King of the Isles had his Residence; his Houses, Chapel, etc. are now ruinous. His Guards de Corps . . . kept Guard on the Lakeside nearest to the Isle', but the 'Walls of their Houses' have disappeared and the castle on the islet is reduced to remnants of its keep and curtain walls. On a neighbouring islet the fourteen chiefs who formed the Council which advised on Hebridean affairs had their headquarters: 'The High Court of Judicature, consisting of Fourteen, sat always here.' It was in this rather barren landscape with the Paps of Jura away to the north that the coronation of the Kings took place in a cer-

Standing Stone

emonial very close to Dunadd's. 'There was a big Stone of seven Foot square, in which there was a deep Impression made to receive the Feet of Mack-Donald; he was crowned King of the Isles standing in this Stone, and swore that he would continue his Vassals in the possession of their Lands and do exact Justice to all his Subjects, and then his Father's Sword was put into his hand.'

Where Finlaggan represented at least an attempt at peaceful rule, Dunyveg Castle was a rallying point for persistent conflict. Now a handsome ruin, it was erected on a promontory at the south-west end of Lagavullin Bay, on two levels joined by a stairway from the

inner courtyard. Parts of the drawbridge are still there, some of the walls, the sea-gate. It is much photographed and used on the cover of Ordnance Survey maps of Islay. It overlooks Texa, the little island with the remains of a medieval chapel where local tradition says Columba made his first landing in Scotland. But Dunyveg's story is strictly secular – a long and sorry tale of internecine quarrels, clan feudings and quarrels with the Crown. Most of what is left of the castle belongs to the sixteenth century when it had already been fought over for two hundred years. There are written records of Dunyveg in the fourteenth century, but it may well be older – built in the twelfth century by Somerled's grandson, Donald, to protect the fleet anchored in Port Ellen. Another two hundred years on, and the MacDonalds still occupied the fortress, remaining as its keepers under James the Fourth though it had been declared a royal castle. His successors were less tolerant and under James the Fifth, Dunyveg came under siege and was garrisoned for a time by the king's troops. But the MacDonalds held on and it was not until the days of James the Sixth that it fell, in 1615, after a lengthy siege and bombardment. It took two hundred men led by General Sir Oliver Lambert and cannon shipped over from Ireland to breach the walls and reduce it. The overall operation was under the command of Sir John Campbell who received the castle and lands on Islay as his reward. There was to be one siege more before the Campbells entered into undisputed possession. Old Colkitto (MacDonald) who had escaped by sea when Dunyveg fell in 1615, had succeeded in recapturing it. During the Civil War and the Montrose campaigns in which his son 'Young Colkitto' played a prominent part, it was forced to surrender to General Leslie and his Roundheads when the water supply ran out. Old Colkitto was hanged, treacherously it is said, and the castle handed back to the Campbells. When they finally moved to the newly built Islay House, they destroyed Dunyveg, the symbol of Mac-Donald power over Islay.

The battles of long ago were by no means fought only against kings and Campbells. In 1598, the rebel Sir James MacDonald had become something of a hero on Islay when he defeated his uncle, the gigantic Lachlan Mor Maclean of Duart at Gruinart. The usual territorial dispute was behind the fighting, and now as then, the rights and wrongs of it are virtually impossible to sort out. But the Battle of Traigh Gruineart is the stuff bards sing of – a grim fairy tale set on the shores of the remote loch which cuts down from the north towards Loch Indaal. Though the Macleans' forces greatly outnumbered the Mac-Donalds', it seems that the day was lost when Lachlan was approached by the Dubh Sith (black fairy), a dwarfish and ill-favoured youth who came to offer his services as an archer. He introduced himself as a Shaw of Jura, but according to the prejudice of the day such misbegotten creatures were thought to be 'spawn of the devil' and Lachlan turned him away. MacDonald was wiser in welcoming him, for in the end it was the Dubh Sith's arrow which killed Maclean. Fate foredoomed the enterprise for Lachlan had ignored the warnings of the wise woman he had consulted before leaving Mull – by landing on a Thursday and by quenching his thirst at a forbidden well. He had also been told that he was not to fight anywhere near Loch Gruinart. The body of the great Lachlan, who was said to be seven feet tall, was carried over the moor past Loch Gorm and buried in Kilchoman church over by Machir Bay. The whole area between the two lochs Gruinart and Gorm is isolated, penetrated only by rough roads. The coast itself with its beautiful stretches of sand is a dangerous one where the strong currents that make bathing dangerous have been responsible for many a wreck. Remote too is the southern area known as the Oa, a lumpy peninsula ending in the Mull where an American war memorial in the shape of a lighthouse was erected to mark the sinking of troop carriers by German U-boats during the First World War. The many remains in these lonely lands – chapels and crosses, duns and standing stones, a possible hut circle, traces of the MacDonalds' summer palace – suggest that once they were active centres of population. Where man moved out the birds have moved in. Fulmars nest in the cliffs of the west coast, corncrakes still chatter in the old crofting land of the Rhinns, the now rare chough, the small crow with its elegant red beak and leggings has made the Oa

174

its territory, every kind of duck including the eider and scoter winter on Loch Indaal. And there are the geese, the Barnacle geese from Greenland who invade its shores in their hundreds. I know of no finer sight, nor of a more unexpected one than a pair of buzzards courting over the moor by the old road near Bridgend.

Birds, and wild flowers, are a special feature of the little island of Gigha – thirty different species counted on pasture land as well as the many varieties of gulls and duck, including eider, who frequent its waters. Mute swans nest there too. They call Gigha the 'good island' or 'God's' depending on how you translate the Old Norse name. The island, six miles long and a mile or two across, is the first landmass one sees on the way to Islay with the islet of Cara at its southern tip. It stays with one for most of the journey to Port Ellen, but there is no way of reaching it

Barnacle Goose

175

GIGHA

KILCHATTAN
ACHAMORE

ARDMINISH
BAY

GIGALUM
ISLAND

CARA

0   3

MILES
APPROX

without returning to the mainland. Small ferries make the three mile crossing two or three times a day; they leave from a jetty half a mile from the pretty village of Tayinloan, itself halfway down Kintyre. Once on Gigha it is another ten minutes walk from the landing stage at Ardminish Bay to the island's only village, with its school, post office and general store. Only part of the population of about 200 lives there, the rest are deployed round and about a dozen farms or so. Gigha is perhaps the most fertile of the Hebrides, 'good for Pasturage and Cultivation' as Martin rightly says. It has produced corn and cattle, as well as its own cheese.

The whole island offers a choice of easy walks: its central hilly ridge enclosing three lochs slopes down through moorland bright with gorse to the creeks and sandy coves of the east coast with lovely views over to the heights of Kintyre; the west side is steeper – fulmars nest in the cliffs which in places drop sheer to the sea. To the north, Gigha ends in a rounded peninsula inaccurately called Eilean Garbh, where the gulls breed; to the south it is prolonged by the tiny islet of Gigalum and a mile further out, by Cara, another deserted island where a late medieval chapel and an empty factor's house dating from the eighteenth century are evidence that it was once inhabited by more than its white goats.

Gigha and Cara came under the rule of the Lords of the Isles and were involved in the quarrels of the MacDonalds and the Campbells – in one dramatic episode, the rebel Sir James based his fleet in Cara during an assault on Kintyre. From the sixteenth century onwards the MacNeills of Gigha were in possession, then the MacNeills of Taynish and Colonsay. They lie buried in the chapel of Kilchattan. The stones in the floor are now grass-grown, but the effigies on the grave slabs can still be distinguished. 'Most of all the Tombs have a two-handed Sword engraved on them, and there is one that has the Representation of a Man upon it.' Martin also noticed what is perhaps Gigha's most interesting, certainly its most unusual, antiquity. 'Near the West-side the Church there is a Stone of about 16 Foot high, and 4 broad, erected upon the eminence.' He could not have realised the singular importance of the

Ogham stone, and his description no longer fits it – several falls have broken its upper end and reduced it to no more than about five feet. Its historical interest lies in the fact that it is engraved with the hieroglyphics of the ancient Ogham script brought over from Ireland by the Dalriads. Scholars agree that it is an early example of a funeral pillar and, from the inscription, that it stands over the body of a prince.

Gigha's long history has left it with many remains of the past, and one modern creation – the magnificent gardens of Achamore House, which can hold their own against any in Scotland. Among their woods, they cover fifty acres with camellias, azaleas, magnolias, rhododendrons and unusually in these parts, roses. Achamore was planned and developed by the late Colonel Sir James Horlick (of the firm that made the popular bed-time drink) who bought the island in 1944. Even on a short visit, it should not be missed.

Gigha has been described, by Nigel Tranter, as a microcosm of the Hebrides. It makes a perfect preface for those setting out on their travels and an unforgettable envoi on the way back from the Inner Hebrides.

Guillemots

VIII
Fine Fare

'Just look at the product of these Highlands' – so wrote William Cobbett, the great agronomist as we should now call him, who in the early 1830s extended his rural rides to Scotland. Atrabilious perhaps by temperament, he was readier to criticise than to praise, but the man who listed forty-four varieties of English eating apples (*The English Gardener, 1833*) knew a good thing when he saw one. 'All that we have heard about this barrenness of the Highlands of Scotland has been most monstrous exaggeration. The Island is good to the very northernmost point of it; one part is good for one thing; another part is good for another thing; but there is in reality nothing bad belonging to it.' To prove his point, Cobbett brought back to exhibit to his doubting London friends 'a beautiful sample of apples' from the Clyde district and 'a cheese of excellent flavour, and of half a hundred weight' bought in Ayrshire.

Like other travellers of his day and before, Cobbett was entertained by the wealthy, by the newly enriched merchants and by the gentry, and roughed it in local inns. He sampled the fare of the privileged and the food of the people. In a country renowned for its fine meat, teeming with game, rich in vegetables and fruit of all sorts, whose waters yield an abundance of fish and crustaceans, he could at

179

least be sure that he was dining on fresh produce, however humble. The difference between the Queen's Soup and the poor man's Barefit (barefoot) Broth is one of cost rather than quality.

Progress has made its inroads, but in spite of the 'fast foods' that have reached every corner of the kingdom courtesy of modern technology, the old tradition of home-grown ingredients prepared with loving skill is not yet lost in Scotland, where soup still comes from the pot rather than the packet.

Potage Lorraine

Also known as Potage à la Reine – the Queen's soup. According to old recipes, this was based on veal stock in which a chicken was cooked, a process which would now raise its price out of reach. A good compromise is to use chicken stock and left-overs of cold chicken as a garnish.

3 pts chicken stock
2 yolks of hard-boiled egg
1 tbs fine white breadcrumbs
¼ pt cream
2 oz almonds
½ lb cold roast chicken
parsley

Moisten the breadcrumbs with a little warm stock and pound them with the egg yolks. Stir in the rest of the heated stock to produce a smooth (velouté) mixture. Blanch the almonds and slice them into thin slivers. Dice the cold meat or mince it and add to the soup. Before serving, stir in the cream (which must not be allowed to boil) and sprinkle with parsley.

Additional seasonings:

A pinch of mace or nutmeg, lemon rind and juice. And for those who prefer a still smoother consistency the almonds and cold meat can be put through the liquidiser along with the breadcrumbs and egg yolks.

This soup was named after James the Fifth's second wife, Mary Queen of Scots' French mother, Marie de Lorraine. The following soup would have been more likely to appear on humbler tables. It too is based on chicken broth – originally provided by that now rare bird, a boiling fowl.

Cock-a-Leekie

The stock:
1½ lbs chicken pieces
3 pts water
carrot, onion, celery
bouquet garni
5 leeks

To prepare the stock, simmer the chicken in the water with the carrot, onion and celery and herbs for at least two hours. Discard the vegetables, remove the meat, then bring to the boil, skim, sieve and remove the fat. This is easier to do if you prepare the stock in advance and allow it to get cold.

Wash the leeks very thoroughly, trim, slice them lengthwise, then cut into pieces 3″ to 4″ long. Cook them in the cleared stock, traditionally seasoned with mace, as well as pepper and salt, for about twenty minutes, and before serving, add the best of the meat cut into convenient pieces.

In old recipes, a handful of prunes were added: they should be soaked, then cooked separately, stoned and added to the stock along with the leeks.

Whether the prunes known in the old days as French plums reflected the French influence on Scottish cooking is a question for the historians of gastronomy to decide, but according to Walter Scott's Meg Dodds, a Cock-a-Leekie in which they figured introduced a banquet served by Lord Holland to the great French diplomat, Talleyrand.

The well-known Scotch Broth bridges the gap between the elegant thin soups of the 'consommé' type and the popular semi-stews.

Scotch Broth

1 lb neck of lamb or chump ends
½ green cabbage
2 carrots
2 turnips
1 leek
1 onion
2 oz split peas
2 oz barley

Cover the meat with cold water (about 3 pints), salt, bring to the boil and skim. Add

the peas and the barley (both soaked overnight and rinsed) and go on cooking for a
couple of hours. The meat will take not more
than an hour; remove it when it is done and
leave aside to cool. Then add the other raw
vegetables, the carrots and turnips diced, the
leek, onion and cabbage shredded; finally the
meat, boned and cut into convenient pieces.

Many traditional Scottish recipes use barley
or rice to give body to the soup; in the following mashed potatoes are used as a thickening.

Scotch Vegetable Soup

1 medium sized floury potato
2 carrots
2 turnips
pieces of celery
2 leeks
1 onion
sorrel if available
2 pts good stock, watered down as necessary

Boil the potato, season and mash with some
of the cooking water to make a thinnish
purée. Add a little butter, but no milk. Cook
the carrots, turnip, onion and celery whole in
the stock till they are soft, then remove and
dice. Meanwhile, add the leeks trimmed and
sliced finely lengthwise, and a handful of
sorrel roughly chopped. When they are done
(about ten minutes) return the diced vegetables to the pan to warm through. Before
serving, stir in a couple of spoonfuls of the
mashed potato. The consistency should
remain that of consommé slightly thickened.

The potato, introduced to the Highlands from Ireland, was not an immediate success. The tale is told of a Clanranald laird who ordered the new tuber to be planted on his estate. In due course, a basket of potatoes was delivered by his tenants who were overheard grumbling that their overlord could make them grow novelties but could not force them to eat them. By the 1840s, however, the potato had become part of the staple diet and the potato famine hit Scotland nearly as badly as it did Ireland. In spite of early prejudice – after all, James the Sixth is said to have hated pork as much as tobacco – so useful and pleasant a vegetable could hardly continue to be ignored as a source of sustenance. Potato (tattie) soup is made in one form or another in many countries; this version uses water and cream instead of stock.

Potato Soup

2 large floury potatoes
2 onions, or 1 onion and 1 leek
¼ pt cream
a little butter

Boil the potatoes (and leek if used) in 2½ pints of salted water till they are soft enough to mash easily. Slice the onion(s) finely and stew slowly without browning in the butter. Sieve (or liquidise) the potatoes, thinning the mash with the cooking water, then add the onions with their juice. Before serving, add the cream and heat through without boiling.

Lentil Soup

6 oz lentils (green or brown)
1 carrot
1 onion
pieces of celery
1 knuckle of bacon or 4 oz piece of streaky
bacon
3 pts water

Having soaked the lentils overnight, bring them slowly to the boil in *unsalted* water along with the bone, then skim. Meanwhile, cut up the other vegetables and fry them briskly in a little butter before adding them to the lentils. Go on cooking gently (for an hour or more) till all are ready to mash. If a piece of bacon is being used to flavour the stock, add it to the vegetables for about half an hour, then remove it and cut it in small pieces to garnish the soup. Thin out the sieved or liquidised vegetables with the cooking liquid; check the seasoning, adding pepper and a little sugar and the bits of bacon. A rich winter soup in which *split peas* can be used instead of lentils.

The vegetables most generally associated with Scotland, kail or cabbage, neeps or turnips, more accurately swedes, come into their own in 'hotch-potch'. Walter Scott's son-in-law and biographer, J. G. Lockhart considered it 'quite peculiar to Scotland', but the word, which entered the English language as early as 1583, is derived from old French for mixing together or jumbling up. And in its current French form, 'hochepot', based on oxtail, remains a popular country dish. In a book of recipes from Scotland, which is also a history of its cuisine, F. Marian McNeill gives hotch-potch its other name of 'Hairst Bree', a harvest broth 'made only when the kail-yard is in its prime, and the soup is piquant with the juices of young growing things. When possible go out with a basket to select your vegetables within an hour or so before starting to prepare them.' The principle is to use twice the weight of vegetables to meat; traditionally the end result should be nearly as thick as porridge. For a meatless soup, a big marrow bone will serve to make the stock; use an oxtail or shin or flank of beef if the meat is to be dished up.

Hotch-Potch

1½ lbs of an inexpensive cut of beef to
3 lbs vegetables
Root vegetables including carrot, turnip, swede, parsnip etc
Green vegetables including 'spring' cabbage, cauliflower, peas, broad beans, lettuce, a few spring onions, parsley to garnish.

Cover the meat with 3 pints of salted water, bring to boil and skim. Cook on for an hour or so, then add the roots cut up into convenient pieces. The hotch-potch can be left on overnight provided the heat can be kept down to a simmer.

The florets of cauliflower are best parboiled separately, then added with the peas and beans during the last hour of slow cooking, along with the lettuce and cabbage, both shredded and (optionally) the spring onion chopped up. Turn out into a tureen and sprinkle with chopped parsley.

If the meat is being used, dish it up in a deep platter surrounded by the vegetables.

Lack of transport in a country where roads have had to be cut through mountains, circumvent long stretches of water and adapt themselves to the jigsaw of the coastline has meant that rich and poor alike have had to be largely self-sufficient. Fish, from the sea, the loch or the burn, has been an important natural resource and played a big part in the national economy. The Scots became, and remain, adept at its preparation, curing, salting, smoking. Fresh fish was served up, grilled, sauced, poached (in both senses of the word) and the noble salmon as well as the humble winkle went into the soup pot, along with barley or oatmeal to thicken the broth and herbs to flavour it. Along the seaboard, crabs provided the traditional

Partan Bree (or Crab Broth)

Most modern cookery books use the recipe originally taken from those collected, and published early this century, by Lady Clark of Tillypronie.

1 crab, cooked
2 oz rice
1 pt milk
¾ pt cream
anchovy paste or essence

Slowly boil the rice in the milk and when it is quite soft add the crab meat after setting aside the claws. Sieve into a basin and thin out with 'white' stock (fish or chicken) if you have it, or with water. Season with (only a little) salt, white pepper and a small spoonful of anchovy paste. Return to the cleaned pan and reheat, adding at the last moment the cream and the claw meat cut into substantial pieces.

The excellence of this soup depends on using fresh crab, but a pleasant substitute can be made with tinned crab, with the addition of a few shrimps or prawns to take the place of the claw meat.

Crab has become something of a luxury; in the old days a recipe which made use of exotic, imported rice as well as cream would have been restricted to the castle rather than the cottage. The following recipe for salmon soup, on the other hand, would have been cheap enough at a time when living-in servants tried to make it a term of their employment that they should not be made to eat salmon, at least not more than twice a week. The ready availability of farmed salmon has now brought it within reach of most purses.

Salmon Soup

About ½ lb salmon steak or tail

For the stock:

1 whiting or two, or other cheap fish
carrot
onion
celery
bouquet garni

cream
fresh parsley
a little potato (or rice) flour

Cover the whiting and vegetables, roughly chopped, with about 2 pts of water, season, bring to the boil, then simmer for an hour. The addition of a glass of white wine may not be classical, but it does a lot for what the French call a 'fumet' or fish stock. Strain through a fine sieve into a clean pan. Poach the salmon in this (for up to 15 minutes, depending on the cut), then remove and thicken the liquid with a scant spoonful of potato flour. Skin and bone the salmon, flake it and add it to the soup, which is finished off with some cream and finely chopped parsley. (Trimmings or smoked salmon cut into slivers will not come amiss.)

All along the Atlantic seaboard, people have made the best use they can of their stores of cod and haddock, salted, smoked or dried for preservation. The Spanish and Portuguese have their bacalaō; the French, their brandades; the Americans, their chowders. Perhaps best of all is the Scots soup, based on smoked haddock, and known as

Cullen Skink

1 lb smoked haddock
2 medium-sized onions, finely chopped
3 large potatoes, peeled and sliced
½ pt milk
2 oz butter
white pepper
salt

Cook the haddock in a saucepan with the water on a low heat for about fifteen minutes, then remove it and put it on a dish and strain the liquid in which it has been cooked into a bowl. Clean the saucepan and add onions, potatoes, (a little) salt and pepper and the liquid from the bowl. Cover the pan and cook until the potatoes are soft. Remove the skin and bones from the fish and flake it. Next remove the potatoes from their pan and mash them up with the onions and cooking liquid, gradually add the milk, stirring until they are well blended. Return the pan to a low heat and add the flaked fish and butter and stir until the mixture is hot.

This recipe was given me by Mrs Prunella Kilbane; it comes from her collection of international recipes.

Shell-fish, particularly the smaller varieties, were little thought of in the Highlands and Islands and used generally as a last resort. Recipes from the Hebrides have, however, been preserved for soups made with winkles, or a mixture of cockles and mussels and razor-fish, based on a simple fish stock or milk and water, thickened with oatmeal. Their chief merit was that with the raw material to be gathered freely along the shore, they were cheap. Mussels, however, gained a certain reputation, giving their name so it seems to Musselburgh, the ancient fishing port which was once a Roman settlement on the coast south of Edinburgh. This modern version of an old recipe recalls

Mussel Brose

2 pts mussels
1 oz butter
½ pt milk
a little flour
dry white wine (optional)
1 onion, chopped
plenty of parsley

Wash and scrub the mussels thoroughly in cold water, especially if they are wild rather than farmed. Put them in a large saucepan with the onion and cover with water or wine and water mixed. Turn up the heat and cook till the shells open. Don't boil or overcook or the mussels will be tough. Remove them and strain the cooking liquid into a basin – you may have to do this several times using a fine sieve to remove all traces of sand. Prepare a white sauce with the butter and flour, adding the milk and thinning it out with the strained cooking liquid. Remove the mussels from their shells and reheat them in the soup, adding a little cream (optional) and parsley chopped finely.

Shell-fish give their full flavour to the soup known the world over as 'bisque'. Though lobster is not a necessary ingredient, it is relatively expensive to make even when using a mixture of prawns, shrimps, scallops etc. But it is worth splashing out occasionally on the following recipe, again provided by Mrs Kilbane who is more than justified in describing it as 'an epicure's delight'.

Bisque of Shell-Fish

For the marinade:

3 pts white wine
¼ pt wine vinegar
3 dsps olive oil
½ carrot, peeled
1 onion, chopped
2 shallots, chopped
white part of 1 leek
juice of half a lemon
garlic, peeled and crushed
bay leaves
parsley

2 lbs chosen fish
3 lbs tomatoes
¼ pt good sherry
½ pt double cream
3 egg yolks

The day before, prepare the marinade, shell the fish and marinade overnight. Next day chop the tomatoes, transfer the fish in its marinade into a saucepan, add tomatoes and simmer gently until cooked. Allow to cool. Remove fish and tomatoes and put through blender. Replace this mixture in the marinade and allow to simmer for 1½ hours, then strain. Just before serving, beat the egg yolks and add to the liquid together with the cream and sherry. Stir well, check seasoning, and serve.

Mrs Kilbane adds: 'It is no good making a small quantity of this soup. The above recipe will make enough for eight and it is so good that I have no doubt your guests will ask for a second helping or certainly want it served again the following day.'

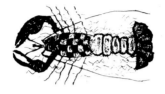

Index of Persons

Index of Persons

196

Index of Places

Index of Places